TWICE FOUND

TWICE FOUND

*Getting a Second Chance at Life, Love,
and Understanding God*

KYLE DUFORD

Foreword by Charlie Peacock
GRAMMY® AWARD-WINNING MUSIC PRODUCER

Estes Press
Greenville, SC

Twice Found is a work of nonfiction.
Some names and identifying details have been changed. This is the best I remember it happening, according to my own memory and consulting with some individuals.

© 2021 by Kyle Duford

Published in Greenville, South Carolina, by Estes Press.

All scripture quotations, unless otherwise indicated, are taken from the *Holy Bible, New International Version®, NIV®*. Copyright ©1973, 1978, 1984, 2011 by Biblica, Inc.™ Used by permission of Zondervan. All rights reserved worldwide. www.zondervan.com. The "NIV" and "New International Version" are trademarks registered in the United States Patent and Trademark Office by Biblica, Inc.™

Other scripture references are from the following sources:

The Message (MSG) by Eugene H. Peterson. © 1993, 1994, 1995, 1996, 2000. Used by permission of NavPress Publishing Group. All rights reserved.

The New Testament in Modern English by J.B Phillips copyright © 1960, 1972 J. B. Phillips. Used by permission of HarperCollins. All rights reserved.

Typeset in Adobe Skolar STD.
Cover design by Chris Heuvel, The Brand Leader (thebrandleader.com)

Library of Congress Control Number: 2021949900
Duford, Kyle
Twice Found: Getting a Second Chance at Life, Love, and Understanding God

ISBN: 978-0-578-32905-5 (paperback)
ISBN: 978-0-578-32042-7 (ebook)

*For Jerushah, my unbelievable wife, who has shown me
Jesus more each day than I thought possible.
FIILU.*

CONTENTS

TWICE FOUND

FOREWARD

It's been an honor to endorse many people and things in my long music career. Not just books and recordings, but software, non-profits, guitars, festivals, and conferences, too. Then there's the rare treat when some writer, one far too trusting, gives you free rein with the foreward of their book.

Your work is to offer both analysis and praise in equal measure. Too much of one or the other, and the whole foreward will tip towards boring or embarrassing oversell. Put all that aside for a minute, though. In my case, with Kyle's book, the approach had to be different. *Why?* I couldn't stand outside this book as an objective observer. *I'm in it*. It's personal.

This book held up a mirror to my life, and I saw my own story afresh. I, too, am twice found. There's an excellent chance you might be too.

A love-hate relationship with a parent you think you're over, but you're not? *Check*. An early run-in with Jesus and the Christian church as a young teenager only to be lost again? *Check*. Take the kind of risks with your life that could quickly lead to death? *Check*. Falling for an amazing woman and almost throwing it all away? *Check*.

There's more, but the point is sufficiently made.

Similar to Kyle's story, the love of God and the love of my life found me—not once but twice. I was given a massive second chance at living. I never thought I'd make it past 20 or 30, let alone live to do more than just survive. Instead, once a twice-lost man, now by faith in the Love that will not let me go, I am extravagantly found.

This, dear readers, is what you will find between the covers of Kyle's honest and newsworthy book.

There's a common misconception among too many people who profess to be Christians. They are all about the good news but have no clue how to act around the news that isn't. Bad news is better left in the past. After all, hasn't Jesus restored all that the locust have eaten? Cast my sins as far as the east is to the west?

Of course. But life isn't a Bible quiz. Bad news is essential too. Why do you think the Bible has so much bad news in it? Thank God that Kyle chose to include a heaping portion in *Twice Found*. And because he did, we can see with clear eyes just how remarkable the Good News actually is.

I'm an artist. I make stuff. Music, paintings, poems, picket fences. I once made a home and recording studio out of a 1910 country church. In all my making, I've kept one essential principle of design in the forefront of my imagination: *the principle of contrast*.

Contrast catches the eye, grabs your attention. Contrast helps our brains organize all the data we're taking in 24/7. Contrast creates focus.

You mix bad news in with the good news, and there's a story worth telling. Not the easy road of information transference, but the messy path of trustworthy, lasting transformation.

In his artful, rambling style, Kyle offers this good outcome in the form of an entertaining and easy-to-read book. He's as good a storyteller as there ever was, each sentence rich with honesty and empathy.

You may find, as I did, that he's telling something of your

story too. I'm counting on it.

A good book like Kyle's has the power to set things right—to administer the second chance. That's not hyperbole. It's recognition of the Spirit of God at work.

The glory shifts back to God alone. The shame is overcome by grace. Love keeps no record of wrongs, and hope is not deferred.

—*Charlie Peacock*
GRAMMY® award-winning music producer
Co-founder, Wedgwood Circle and Art House America
Nashville, Tennessee
October 2021

INTRODUCTION
BOND, JAMES BOND
"I am forgotten as though I were dead;
I have become like broken pottery." —Psalm 31:12

I had been riding my first bike for about a year. I got it when I turned nine years old, and I didn't look back: a brand-new 1983 Schwinn Predator Chromoly BMX-style bike with checkerboard pads that covered the top-tube, stem, and handlebar. It was a single-speed bike with a freewheel hub and a single brake lever on the right side of the handlebar. I zip-tied a 007 number plate on the front of it, and I would pretend to be Roger Moore playing James Bond in *Moonraker, For Your Eyes Only,* or *Octopussy*—Bond movies my brother would let me watch without telling our mother.

Watching my local friends and me tool around on our BMXs in our little sub-division of townhouses in West Allentown, Pennsylvania, would look like a scene from *Stranger Things.* We tore up those roads on our bikes, riding up and down the hills, jumping curbs with makeshift ramps made from leftover construction site wood, and hooting and hollering like little wolverines in the wild. There were no rules: our squad of four or five self-governed itself, alternating who decided where we'd ride that day—the choices were slim—and whether to ride BMX bikes or Santa Cruz skateboards—the bikes usually won out. We never fought.

That summer, everywhere I went, I wore a pair of Vans checkerboard slip-ons that matched my bike. Saturday mornings, I'd leave the house with a belly full of Frosted Flakes and be gone until dusk. In those days, kids could leave for hours as long as you "didn't leave the neighborhood." I was gone every weekend and on school nights until the time changed or it got too cold.

One morning toward the end of the summer of '84, I woke up, rode out to the squad meeting place, and waited while seated on my bike how I imagined James Dean would've sat if he'd rode my Schwinn and not his Porsche Spyder: one arm up on the handlebar, a smirk on his face.

A few minutes went by, and then a few more. I didn't have a watch, but I could tell the day was moving because, from my vantage point, I could see the volume of cars on Walbert Avenue, the main artery through our side of town.

I decided to ride past Andy's house. No one. I went by Ryan's house. Same story. I rode up and down Chalmette Avenue in my little sub-division a dozen times, looking for signs of life. No one, at least under ten years old, was around.

Then I heard a few kids laugh and looked to see where the sound was coming from. I turned my little chrome beast in that direction and took off toward the playground situated in the middle of Country Crossings.

The park was vacant minutes earlier, but now there were three BMX bikes on their sides like horses lying down in a meadow, all scattered on the grassy hill nearby, and one bigger bike in the same position: on its side, in the grass, aimed in a readiness position to take off like a fighter jet on an aircraft carrier.

I knew that bike. It was Chris Cray's, the older neighborhood kid who hated me because someone told him I wrote "Chris Cray is gay" on the park's slide. I hadn't. He didn't care.

All my friends were sitting *under* that same slide now, looking at me from behind that wide metal sheet, laughing. Somehow, in the dark hours between last night and this morning's bowl of cereal, I had been replaced.

"What are you doing here, doofus?" called one of my former friends, riffing off my last name.

"Guys . . .?" I sheepishly replied, one leg propped on a pedal and the other on the ground.

"Doofus, doofus, what a goofus!"

I didn't stay for anymore. I stood up on my pedal to thrust my bike forward and zoomed down the hill, into my yard, and inside. We never rode together again.

That day ended up being filled with cartoons rather than biking, but in my sadness, I realized something: I still had my bike. They hadn't stolen *that* from me.

On subsequent days I would follow the same old routine: wake up, cartoons, Frosted Flakes, and out the door. But now I was a pack of one—a lone wolf, wild and free.

As a poster child for latchkey kids of the 80s, I found independence fairly familiar. I found my own scrap wood and created makeshift jumps. I would ride up and down the main drag jumping the curbs, and I'd whiz back down to my house at the end of the day, full of pride at my accomplishments.

Being on a bike was my escape from feeling like I was a letdown to others. I didn't need anyone else to ride with. This wasn't like being kicked off of a baseball team with no one to play catch. All I needed to do was pedal my little Vans-adorned feet and my bike would take me away.

It was my freedom.

One summer, a few years later, when I was about twelve years old, a new kid started at the summer camp I attended: Joshua. The new kids always had it good in school, like a new flavor of Baskin-Robbins ice cream, but at summer camp, we were all equal. He not only assimilated into our group, but we became fast friends. He was slender with olive skin and piercing, slanting eyes that made him look half-Asian or exotic somehow, even though he was from Virginia and an all-American mutt like me, I thought. Later I found out he had Asian ancestors. By the time summer had ended, he had already shared my birthday party, summer overnights, and countless bonfires under the open night sky while at the camp.

When the school year came, Josh remarkably was there on the first day. We high-fived in the hallway, caught up since the last time we'd seen each other, and then moved on to our homerooms. Unfortunately, we didn't share the same homeroom, but rather he shared his with guys like Ryan and Andy. Eventually, they all became friends, and not surprisingly, part of the exclusive popular kids' crowd, skateboards and all.

One day their newly formed group passed me while I was riding alone in the neighborhood, dreaming up imaginative stories in my head and acting them out on my bike. One of the kids yelled "Doofus" at me as I pedaled on by, but then I heard something else.

"Hey!" said a voice sternly. "Leave him alone. He's my friend." It was Josh.

Over the course of my life, my current bike was always my best friend, or so I thought. Riding was always my escape, my freedom. It took me far away from my present difficult situation. I could lose myself on those wheels, and I did.

I was lost and didn't know it. I thought I was looking for

someone, but rather, I was the person being chased.

I recently realized that God had given me this gift of cycling to pull me back to him. The thrill of the ride was to show me the thrill I could have in Jesus. The feeling of the wind in my face was the same feeling of the wild freedom I now have in Christ. And that person I was chasing—or thought I was chasing—was actually chasing me. Jesus was with me at every point of my life's five-decade race. He pursued me through my love of everything outdoors. As the creator of all things, he manifested himself in the creation I loved and enjoyed. He also showed me himself through the many people along the way disguised as "Jesus with skin on," as my wife says. Josh was one of them.

I first met God as a teenager, but soon after, I began a life of pretending to be someone else. I didn't understand that God loved me as I was. I wore many masks and sought identity in the wrong things. Even in the lowest parts of my life race, the time when I thought I couldn't finish, he was there calling for me, just as I was. In fact, when I was at my lowest, broken and alone, it was there that he found me for the second time—caught me!

When I use the term "broken," I'm referring to the state of surrender to the Lord in which we enter after experiencing hardship and defeat, most of the time the result of our own transgressions. It's only once we are broken, like David describes in Psalm 31, that we are actually ready to be molded back anew. Once I realized that truth—that I was sinful and in need of God's intervention—I was able to continue the race, but this time with Jesus by my side.

Not only did I find Jesus, but I also found the love of my life, the very woman who showed Jesus to me when I needed her most. I will be eternally thankful for this tailormade gift for me from God.

These days, I ride just for fun, not to escape or be free, because I already am, in Christ. And I no longer pursue the empty, unfulfilling things of this world or an identity that is not my own. I'm done with that rat race because I found God.

I'm no longer lost, but I've been found—twice.

And this is my story.

1 | JUST PLAIN

"Just to be is a blessing. Just to live is holy."
—Rabbi Abraham Joshua Heschel

I didn't grow up religious. My mother had vowed to raise her three children without pushing an agenda on them like her mother did with Catholicism. (When she went to college, she still thought she could get pregnant if she sat on a toilet after a man did.) She vowed never to raise us like that. So there was no mention of God or the afterlife. In fact, if there were mention of Jesus, it was as a curse word. I remember learning it was a *bad* curse word when I was ten years old and my mother smacked me for saying his name. I didn't learn he was a *person* until I was sixteen.

We lived quite modestly with my older brother, Christian, my older sister, Allyson, and my mom—who kept my father's last name even though he left when I was two years old. Our mother earned a low-wage salary in social work, yet we lived in an affluent, trendy area of West Allentown in a new townhouse—a gift from my father when he took off and left her the old single-family house to sell and keep the profits. It was here in the West side of this Billy-Joelsong-title-of-a-town where most of the Jewish families lived, and as a result, most of my friends were Jewish. I was jealous of them. Bar mitzvahs and Hanukkah seemed not just like fun days but purposeful. Learning their Hebrew scriptures and memorizing those lines before they turned of age was oddly fascinating to me, and I watched it all from the sidelines. But I also secretly knew it was something I wanted to experience.

Christian went to Boston University when I was six, and Ally left to enroll in Carnegie Mellon in Pittsburgh when I was nine. Because daycares were expensive, especially in the summer, my mother didn't know what to do with me. Sometimes, during in-school holidays or parent-teacher days, I'd go to work with her, but mostly I was left alone, fending for myself. Summers, however, were the hardest.

During the summers, I spent ample time with my mother's parents, who we called Nanny and Bacca, my brother's name for my grandfather when he was three and it just stuck. Living with them for the entirety of summer wasn't doable—partly because it was important for me to have social interactions at that age, but also because they were also growing older, and it was harder for them to care for me for long stints. So, I spent the first two weeks and the last two weeks of summer with them. In between, my mother found a solution for the costly daycare issue: the Jewish Community Center Day Camp, which offered an eight o'clock to three o'clock camp day, much like school hours. It was a bonus that I'd be home by three-thirty because I'd be on my BMX bike, pretending to be James Bond in an Aston Martin by four. But it was even more of a bonus to learn of this fascinating religion from my new friends.

The days I attended camp, I would take a bus from outside my home to the Allentown Jewish Community Center Day Camp roughly fifteen miles away in Coopersburg, Pennsylvania, where my grandparents lived. At the end of each day, I'd ride a school bus home to our little townhouse. On the rare occasion I had to go to

Nanny and Bacca's, I'd take a different bus just five minutes down the road, and Bacca would pick me up at the stop outside of Madle's Hardware. For my mother, these summer days were mostly like any day the rest of the year. She could work, knowing I was not just safe but doing *something*. Ride the bus in the morning; ride the bus in the evening. Jump on my bike. Repeat.

The JCC was where I learned team sports like football, baseball, soccer, hockey, and a few individual ones like swimming and archery. We played kick the can and made friendship bracelets. In between, we'd learn arts and crafts in the art pavilion and make-up songs that began "arts and farts and toilet parts." It was great. From the time we got off the bus in the morning until we left at three o'clock in the afternoon, I was either covered in sweat or wet from the outdoor pool.

My mother would pack my lunch: big plums nearly twice the size of my mouth that were so juicy the nectar would roll down my chin in the hot summer sun. Then I'd eat the pre-cooked kosher hotdogs and drink this fantastic orange drink from milk cartons that they had in big coolers outside the pavilion. We could pick milk, chocolate milk, or this orange stuff. What was that drink? I can't remember, but it was amazing. On the occasional overnight event, we'd cook our dogs and s'mores over a campfire.

Every Friday, we celebrated the Sabbath by eating challah bread and ice cream while singing acoustic Beatles' songs like "Bungalow Bill" and "Maxwell's Silver Hammer" with head counselor, Mickey Freeman, playing acoustic guitar and leading us in song. I knew all the words by heart to "Maxwell's Silver Hammer," and we'd laugh each time we'd yell "bang, bang" or "clang, clang," whichever the chorus warranted.

Then after it was all said and done, we'd end each camp day sitting on the hot pavilion concrete, legs folded to sing "Taps" a cappella as a group with Mickey leading us:

Day is done.
Gone the sun.
Gone the lake, gone the hills, gone the sky.
All is well, safely rest.
God is nigh.

We thought for years we were singing "God is nice" because that made sense to us. I mean, he made archery, ice cream, and The Beatles, so he must be nice, right? Sure, he never magically turned me into a James—Bond or Dean—or into the brother of some television character when I prayed, but I came close in my imagination: one day, I was a Klein brother, a Goldberg brother the next. No license to kill, but I belonged with my people. We were brothers in our own exodus in Coopersburg learning to play street hockey on a basketball court—and I loved it.

Because of that sense of belonging I felt, I learned all the prayers and learned how to open meals with "Barukh ata Adonai Eloheinu, melekh ha'olam." But even though I learned their ways, and no matter how much I tried to assimilate myself into this fantastic culture, I knew I would always be on the outside looking in. This was when God, in all his wondrous ways, started to seem foreign to me. My friends had these fun rituals and activities they gladly taught to me, but I failed to comprehend its significance while they persisted in it themselves. I saw nothing different in them than in me—we shot the same arrows and swam in the same pool—but I knew I was still looking at a world from the cold side of frosted windowpanes. They were dancing in the warmth of Yahweh while I was failing to understand the meaning of it all. *Let's just sing more "Ob-La-Di, Ob-La-Da,"* I thought. It was the best I could do.

Mickey would help me through my elementary years. I had always thought he was the son of local legend, Judy Freeman, whose local PBS broadcast kids' show *Hatchy Malatchy* was a 1970s staple in every Allentown home with a television. At least that's how my mother got me to go to day camp. *Oh, his mother was "Miss Judy?" I'll go!* But while the character on that show was called by the same moniker, she was played by an actress. He was, however, the son of Jewish immigrant, who once taught my daycare. Besides, Mickey was happier with a gaggle of children around him than being a pseudo-celebrity in a studio.

"It's okay that you're not Jewish," he told me. "You're still one of God's children." I didn't get it.

Mickey gave my grandmother recipes for hamantaschen—the Jewish jelly-filled cookies I loved—and made me a homemade yarmulke for my head covering and told me to call it a "kippah" if I wanted to fit in, and I desperately wanted that, so I did.

Once a week, when we had music in the "lodge" on campus, we were ecstatic, as the lodge was the only air-conditioned building on the property. We were such turds. When we sang "Three Jolly Fisherman," we'd emphasize the word *damn* when we sang, "They all went down to Amster*dam!*" Afterward, Mickey would tell me the stories of Isaac and Abraham, Noah, and Daniel. I was mesmerized.

My favorite story was David and Goliath. There was something great about using a slingshot and a small rock to level a giant. My mind drifted. *Could I use a slingshot on the older neighborhood kids?* This David seemed remarkable. Small, but brave. And he became a king? Whoa.

As the school years ticked by, I grew accustomed to the rhythm: fall school, winter break, spring with more school, and summer day camp. I yearned for those days in summer, wanting not only to escape the mundaneness of my school days and the neighborhood kids but also to hear more of this mysterious religion. Those were the days to sing songs and break the twisted, soft egg challah bread; to find hot dogs in the grocery store stamped with a

K to make sure they were kosher—just to wrap them individually in aluminum foil and cook them with a stick over a campfire on our overnights, and to have that mystical orange drink each day at lunch in the hot Pennsylvania sun. What *was* that drink called?

Then one day, I asked my mom, "Am I Jewish, or am I *just plain?*"

She laughed from the next room. "Oh, you're just plain," she said and laughed again at the seeming absurdity of my question, not wanting to encourage my Jewish interests and holding fast that she wouldn't raise us with religion.

There I was. Just plain. It validated everything I thought. I was regular. I definitely wasn't James Bond, but I also wasn't even a Goldberg.

In those days, I started to feel and understand what Blaise Pascal meant by having a God-shaped hole in one's life. I just didn't know who Blaise Pascal was just yet. Or, for that matter, God.

I was embarrassed to ask anyone but Mickey any questions or to engage with anyone but him to try to understand religion. I didn't want to expose myself as a non-Jew. It was our secret, Mickey's and mine. I would continue to play the games and do the crafts, sure, but not be seen too much. It was bad enough my name didn't fit in on the daily roll call, somewhere between Mike Abrams and Eli Goldberg. "Duford" definitely did not scream "chosen people."

I went to the JCC Day Camp each summer until I turned fifteen. Mickey was still there, singing his Beatles' songs and teaching kids about Abraham through it all. Along the way, my friends all got bar mitzvahed while I watched from the sidelines and entered my teenage years. Each year, I hid more than just my non-Jewish name and my absent faith; I started to hide from God himself, afraid I was never to be great, chosen, or like David. I'd always be just plain.

2 | THE THIRD CAT
"My sheep listen to my voice;
I know them, and they follow me."
—John 10:27

Bacca, my maternal grandfather, was interesting. He was nearly six feet tall and had thin blondish-red hair and a smile that used to knock the socks off women in the 1930s. He wasn't too shabby as an older man, either. Obsessed with good health, he would hang himself upside down every day for twenty minutes to "reduce the effects of gravity on his wrinkles" and sprinkle lecithin on everything from pancakes to *pite chellia*, the Albanian fried bread dough my grandmother made for us and insisted on calling by its native name. Back then, we didn't know lecithin would one day be used to treat memory disorders such as dementia and Alzheimer's. He was also a genius by definition, held in high regard by engineers because he invented, co-invented, or patented many electronic devices we use today. But he never talked about that. Heck, he never talked about much that was real.

He would tell us stories about growing up in Alsace, France, with his two brothers on a farm with a pig that weighed exactly 321 pounds. He told us of the kid who got super fat because he ate too much vitamin C and that his school was up the other side of a monstrous hill, across a valley. Therefore, each day he had to go downhill first, then up a steep hill to go to school, and logically, he had a similar struggle on the way home.

All lies.

He was actually born in Long Island but would tell these tall tales so well that the movie *Big Fish* could've been about him. He was more Scottish in descent than any part French, although he did speak and read French fluently. He refused to read his Georges Simenon books about the fictional French detective Jules Maigret in any other language than its native tongue. There were always two books on his nightstand: a Maigret novel and an English-French dictionary.

His first wife had abruptly committed suicide but not before she had two children, facts we did not learn until adulthood and that no one ever spoke of. With a demanding job at Bell Labs as a head engineer, he was often forced to leave his two young children with his brother's Albanian wife while he worked. One day when picking up his children, his sister-in-law's younger sister answered the door, and they fell in love at first sight. However, the first fifteen years of my life, I thought he drove by the Faraco estate in a convertible and tried to lasso a daughter and—according to him—lassoed the wrong one. In the end, two brothers married two sisters, forever making my family tree diagram in elementary school not only the most complicated in the class but also the most unbelievable. Shortly after their wedding, they had their first and only child together— his third—my mother.

Since 1940—the same year my mother was born—they had lived in the same house he had designed. It was on eight acres, which my grandmother mowed herself, topless, mind you, on a large Cub Cadet tractor. Over the years, they had seen their children grow up and move on and wished they had company, which was why they enjoyed mine so much. Then one fall, a friend of my grandparents brought them a feral farm cat as a gift. They not only accepted this black ball of fuzz but with my grandfather's penchant for French, they also named it *Chat Trois*—literally "cat three." They were overjoyed.

They loved that cat.

As an eleven-year-old at my grandparents', I made great efforts to endear myself to Chat Trois. I would attempt to catch her, pet her, hug her, love on her—whatever she would tolerate. But she would have none of it. As a somewhat feral kitten, she grew up to be an outdoor mouse hunter that didn't like young boys one bit. I'd get her into a corner, go in for the hug, and—*swack!*—a swipe to my arm with her claws would draw blood from one arm. I'd go back the other way and—*swack!*—again to my other arm. That was our dance, Chat Trois's and mine, but I never gave up. Once, when I was actually able to snag her, she bit through the webbing of my right hand between my thumb and forefinger and brought up her hind legs to push off my little arm. The result looked like I was in an alley fight from *West Side Story*. I was bloodied and hurt but not deterred. I'd go back time and time again and get the same result: swack!

Chat Trois, despite being so unsociable toward me, had a strange ritual with my grandfather. After dinner, Bacca would lay on the living room floor, with his head propped up against the sofa. He'd whistle, and immediately, that devil of a feline would gingerly walk over, hop onto his chest, and curl up as he rubbed her ears. She loved it. She'd purr and purr until both of them fell asleep.

I loved that cat, but she didn't love me. She knew her master.

She knew my grandfather's whistle and his gentle touch. She knew the scratches meant naptime. Even if it was storming, thundering, and lightning, Chat Trois would come in for dinner, knowing her time with Bacca was special. Nothing would stop that cat from getting home.

Just like Chat Trois, we know that Jesus is our master, and if we're saved, we can hear his call, too. He is the shepherd, and we are his sheep: "His sheep follow him because they know his voice. But they will never follow a stranger; in fact, they will run away from him because they do not recognize a stranger's voice" (Jn 10:4b) "His sheep follow him because they know his voice. But they will never follow a stranger; in fact, they will run away from him because they do not recognize a stranger's voice" (-5). I was a stranger to Chat Trois. No wonder she avoided me.

But like that cat, I followed a familiar voice—my own "voice" as a kid, although I became aware there was someone else out there, someone to whom I was drawn, someone who made sense to me. I wasn't sure who it was yet. Someone was calling me. It wasn't my absent father's voice nor my stressed and overwhelmed mother's voice, either.

I, like that cat, wanted to be in the same room as other people but not interact with them. I wanted to be free and wild but come home for dinner. I was, in a sense, feral myself. I was wild for life but wouldn't give people the time of day. I looked friendly, but man, don't try to talk to me, or I may scratch or—*swack!*—worse. I had a way of putting people down to make myself look good, if only to myself. I was a paradox, for sure. I wanted structure and rules, but I wanted to be let go and free. I was wild at the core, and I didn't come when I was called. I didn't recognize or trust the voice calling me.

Would there ever be a time when I would hear my name called out and everything would be fine, safe, and cozy? Would I be nourished and well taken care of but allowed to be "me?" Would I ever nap soundly? It would be a while before I was broken enough to hear and respond to my call from Jesus.

3 | THE SPELLER

"There are different kinds of gifts, but the same Spirit distributes them." —1 Corinthians 12:4

No matter my age, I always wished for a different life. I was ten years old when I would sit up at night in bed and pray that when I woke up in the morning, I would be a Duke brother. I would've even accepted a cousin, somehow related to Bo and Luke from the *Dukes of Hazzard*—or at least to have woken up in their world. I would imagine myself riding in the back of their customized 1969 orange Dodge Charger, the General Lee, to bear witness to all their antics throughout Hazzard County. In these dreams, however, I just never knew how to get into the back seat with those doors welded shut and all. My Jewish friends made me think it didn't work that way, but I tried, nevertheless.

My family never went to church, so these magic transformation requests were the only times I prayed as a child unless it was a blessing at day camp. I didn't know what prayer specifically was—all I knew were standardized Jewish blessings—but I hoped whoever was listening—to whatever I was asking for—would grant just one wish. Any one of them would do. I guess I thought that if you said your wishful prayer enough times, some genie somewhere heard you and granted your request.

By age twelve, I wanted to be Sven, the blue lion robot pilot and member of *Voltron*—a cartoon about five lion robots that would unify into an even larger robot that fought intergalactic evil. Space fighting robots seemed perfect.

If I couldn't change who I was, I at least wanted to change my name from Kyle to anything else. Sven sounded like a good one. In addition to the bike gang calling me "doofus," everyone else gave me nicknames, too, from my grandmother, who called me "Kyla," to my dad, who called me "Ky," which I didn't like. I wouldn't have minded if it was spelled "Kai" because then I could pretend I was a Japanese samurai. Even my classmates had a nickname for me. A friend at school got his Tandy TRS-80 computer to pronounce the names of kids in class. Mine came back as "Kulu," and he called me that until college. I was bored with my name, and I hated family nicknames.

All that year, I came home alone since my siblings had both left for college. I was sad and especially discontented in my last year of elementary school, sixth grade. I was turning twelve that summer, and my mother immediately thought to have me tested to see if I had attention deficit hyperactivity disorder. It was the new trend back then to diagnose all kids with this—"Oh, they must have ADHD!" She set up an appointment and asked my father to take me to get tested so she'd know how to enroll me in the upcoming seventh grade in Springhouse Junior High School.

He picked me up from summer camp early one day in his convertible Ford Mustang and drove with the top down all the way to Kernsville Elementary School, which looked abandoned in late June.

Once settled at the school, I started to take a series of tests: mazes, puzzles, and word problems. It was annoying to jump from one thing to another, and the room was freezing, which didn't help. I frantically bent my Gumby figurine my grandmother had given me for good luck under the table. It didn't offer solace.

Suddenly, we were finished. I had no idea how I did or how evident it was that I had ADHD. I guessed I failed. I'll never forget walking outside and feeling the warm sun hit me and warm me up. I jumped into the Mustang, and we whizzed away.

My father dropped me off, and I ran up the stairs to the front door of our townhouse. My mother was sitting on the stoop, smoking a cigarette which she extinguished on the cement step next to her into a pile of ash as I approached. She was giving me a look like I'd never seen.

"What?" I said.

"You did it!"

"I have a disorder? I have ADHD?"

"No! You're gifted, silly!"

"'I'm what?" I said. "What does that mean?"

"You're *smart!*" she emphatically said, beaming at her youngest son. "You get to go into different classes next year!" She told me I got a 121 on my IQ test—*not an ADHD test!*—and the school psychiatrist wanted me to go into a different class that fall. My boredom, according to her and the man doing the test, was apparently due to my capacity to learn more, and up until now, classes "hadn't been stimulating enough." That was going to change, she told me. I was pissed she had lied to me about the purpose behind the test.

Going into junior high, I wasn't particularly good at anything. I could ride a bike, sure, but I couldn't skateboard. I didn't watch football or baseball—I definitely couldn't play them. I lacked any real skill. I tried musical instruments like drums, but all I could do was play the *A-Team* theme song. I tried bass guitar, but all I learned was "Spinning Wheel" by Blood, Sweat, and Tears—all you had to do was play the open strings from the top-down: E-E-A-A-D-D-G-G. My sister got all the art skills from my grandmother, and my brother got the gift of languages and now speaks over a half-dozen fluently.

Apparently, there were no more talents left for me, and I

definitely wasn't a good student. So entering school that fall, I was in for a rude awakening. It was daily studying and homework, or I would fall way behind and quickly. The teachers—Mr. Arbogast for geography, Mr. Tannery for English, and Mr. Schaffer for math—all took exceptional care of me. They had to, I was failing miserably, and they all wanted to get to know me in the hope they could help me succeed and perform at my best. School had gone from far too easy to far too hard all because of a stupid test score, and now I was out of my comfort zone. I was most certainly out of my league. *Please God, when I wake up, I want to be Michael from* Knight Rider.

For English, Mr. Tannery took extra steps to help me. He was gray-haired and fit, with muscles about to pop out of his dress shirts. He wore glasses and looked like he came right out of *The Official Preppy Handbook*. His dress shirts were always a pale color of light blue, salmon, yellow, or white, but his pants? They were something else. Madras or plaid, they were loud, bright, and always matched his Timex Expedition watch band. He must've had hundreds of those bands, as he literally changed them every day.

Tannery had invented a character he called "The Speller," a bumbling hero he used to teach us everything we needed to know. He hand-drew these caricatures of this guy who looked suspiciously like him but "super." He'd pin lessons on the bulletin board as if The Speller himself were writing them, as if he knew nothing of it. Tannery made things more fun for seventh-graders studying English, that was certain.

Mr. Tannery knew if it weren't fun, we wouldn't learn. A local newspaper even wrote of him in 1988 that "Tannery pushed his students to their potential, yet they thought they were having fun." I was no exception.

Somehow, he knew that the fifteen or so vocabulary words I needed to memorize each week were a struggle for me, even with The Speller to help me. So he made me a deal—write a new, original story each week and use all those weekly vocabulary words correctly, and he'd pass me.

He started working with me, helping me craft my story and present it to the class. Because of how well I delivered my new, imaginative short stories, he also challenged me to think about acting and eventually gave me the lead in the school play over much more qualified future thespians who would later study acting in New York.

He believed in me that year and many years after. He followed my progress through middle school and would often help edit my creative writing. That guy was a hero to me, and although I was wearing my watch on my right wrist—I wanted to be like Bruce Willis in *Moonlighting*—the watch band I wore every day was now Madras. Today, I still change my Apple watch band often.

I was imaginative as a kid, and although most adults may not have recognized that characteristic as a gift in a child, he was the one who pushed me to channel and hone my imagination into a career. In fact, he even helped me in college with a film script I wrote—that never went anywhere—and encouraged me to always think creatively and not let people tell me I couldn't do anything.

I didn't know I could use my weaknesses for something creative. Tannery's use of The Speller uncovered a desire for storytelling in me, which would ultimately direct my career in magazines, online content, and brand positioning. Tannery saw my potential, and by using The Speller as his tool, he made learning fun. It wasn't drudgery; it was exciting. Through something I didn't understand, I was able to see my gift buried deep inside. Through perseverance, I was able to use the gifts I didn't know I had.

Mr. Tannery didn't help only me and therefore ignore the needs of others in my seventh-grade class; rather, he helped other students as well, all in a uniquely different way from me.

I believe God thinks the same way as Mr. T. did. He takes an interest in us personally, gives us the desires of our hearts (Ps 37:4), and assigns gifts to each of us uniquely (Rom 12:6). He simultaneously looks at each of us individually as special, yet he cares for us all collectively. The gifts he gives us are not just from the Spirit, but they're meant to show him off to others.

He also picks the most unlikely of bumbling heroes to mature into men to be used for his work: Moses before he was the leader of Israel, David before he was king, and The Speller to help lead a young boy into his future.

Mr. Tannery has long since retired, but his stories live on. On Facebook, there are pages dedicated to him and comments like, "When I grow up, I want to be Mr. Tannery." He touched the lives of countless students over forty years of teaching. His patience was extraordinary. His kindness was heartfelt. I'm not sure how he felt about the Lord or if he had faith at all. However, Jesus used him in my life to show me how he created me in his image with certain gifts to be a unique creation he loved.

4 | THE ENTREPRENEUR & THE XEROX MAN

"Anyone who does anything to help a child in his life is a hero." —Fred Rogers

I was fourteen years old when I spotted a guy walking around our neighborhood of Country Crossings with a golden retriever one fall. He looked like a fun guy—to be fair, any guy walking his dog looked cool to a fatherless fourteen-year-old boy—and his yellow, fluffy, obedient dog was beautiful.

I would try to be in the kitchen each afternoon after school to see if I could catch him and his dog walking around. Then one day, about a month after first seeing him, while I was outside playing, I saw him rounding the corner of Chalmette Road onto Yellowstone Road.

As he neared the house, I spoke up, "I like your dog!"

"Thanks," he said. "This is Noelle." Noelle didn't say anything. "I'm Brian," he said.

"I'm Kyle. I live right there," and I pointed to the second townhome from the corner.

"Hi, Kyle," he said and reached out to shake my hand.

"Mind if I walk with you and Noelle for a while?"

"If it's okay with your parents," said Brian.

"It's okay. She doesn't mind." Translation: *She's never home anyway. I'm good.*

I walked down Yellowstone with him as far as I could go before losing sight of my house and then decided to turn around. We exchanged niceties, and I ran back home.

Each day that I saw Brian and Noelle, I'd go a little farther with them. Each time I went a little farther, Brian and I would talk more.

He was twenty-six years old and newly married to his wife, Lynn, a local professor. Brian was a new executive at a local Xerox office and sold copiers to medium-sized businesses and local schools within our district. Each Tuesday and Thursday night, while Lynn was teaching, he was on his own. With my mother's permission, we would combine our leftovers into some strange meal and scarf it down before walking Noelle around the neighborhood—now the entire rectangle of nearly a mile.

On those dinners and long dog walks, Brian would ask me tons of questions, none of which I knew the answers to. He must've suspected the lack of a father figure in my life and taken up the role. He ended up teaching me how to protect myself, defend myself, and throw my first punch. "Warn the guy three times," he said, "and before you get the third warning out, knock his block off—he'll never see it coming." Later, in tenth grade, when a kid started singing, "Rollin', Rollin', Rollin', . . . Rawhide!" replacing "Rollin'" with "Roland," my middle name—and my father's first name—I used Brian's technique. He was right; he never suspected I would throw that punch. I laid him out cold. He never bothered me again.

Brian also taught me how to ask out a girl, how to be kind to her, what to say, and when to kiss her goodnight. When I went to the winter dance at our junior high in eighth grade, he was the one who got credit for my gentlemanly technique. I opened my date's door, bought her a corsage, successfully pinned it on her, and led her onto the dance floor with confidence.

He showed me how to lift weights—and taught me what a bench press even was—how to throw and catch a football, and what all the innuendos on *Coach* meant when we watched it on weeknights. He and Lynn were wildly gracious and welcoming. They sensed I had no one at home and figured, "Why not help this kid out?" I definitely grew to love them, and—looking back on my own life—I can't imagine being a newly married, twenty-six-year-old who wanted to care for a kid half my age. He didn't think twice about it.

When summertime rolled around, Brian suspected I wanted to make some of my own money, and we racked our brains to come up with a plan that wasn't predicated on needing transportation.

"Do you know how to cut grass?" he said.

"Yeah, my mother makes me cut the grass each week."

"Do you like it?"

"Well, I don't know . . ." I said.

"Would you like it if you were paid for it?"

"Der," I said.

"Here's what I'm thinking. There are maybe two hundred townhomes in this development? Easy. Maybe two hundred fifty?"

"Okay . . ."

"If you charge ten dollars per mow and maybe fifteen for end units, I bet you could make a pretty penny."

"I like that," I said. "But I'd need gas and maybe a weed whacker."

"And business cards," Brian said. "I can help you with those at the office."

"Okay, so what do we do now?" I asked.

"We're going to make you some money this summer," he said. "That's what we're gonna do."

He had me at *money*.

"Come on," he said. "Let's come up with a name."

Kyle's West End Lawn Care debuted in May of 1988. The slogan was *"Anytime, anyplace, you'll thank me with a happy face."* This unfortunate tagline, as you can imagine, inspired my older brother to tease me about my unintentional prostitution innuendo, but it did the job. My business launched with an 8.5 x 11-inch flyer, hand-delivered to everyone in the neighborhood. It read:

Kyle's West End Lawn Care
Mowing, Trimming, Bagging, Weeding
Townhomes: $10
End-unit Townhomes: $15
Single-family Homes: $20
Anytime, anyplace, you'll
thank me with a happy face.

The smiley face was my idea.

By hand-delivering each one, I was able to make notes on accepted flyers, rejected flyers, and no-contact mailbox drop-off flyers. If I hadn't heard from the homes with a leave-behind, I re-visited them at a different time of the day the following week and repeated the process.

The landline in my bedroom started ringing off the hook and going to my answering machine, which played the recording, "Hello, you've reached Kyle's West End Lawn Care. Please leave a message, and after our busy day mowing, we'll return your call. Remember, any time, any place, you'll thank me with a happy face. *Beep.*" Within a day, I had ten customers wanting cuts every other week. Then I added ten more and fit them in the odd weeks. Before I knew it, I was earning $400 a month for a few hours of work. Some of them were end units and took me about ten extra minutes than a middle unit, but I earned the extra $5 per lawn.

Brian encouraged me to go to a local print shop and have them make me plain-white cardstock doorknob hangers for when I completed a job. His copiers couldn't make cuts like a print shop could. On these hangers, I'd write out the date the customer's mow was completed, services provided, any other notes that were needed (e.g., "A small litter of newborn rabbits was found near the fence, so I didn't weed whack that section"), and signed each one with a "See you in two weeks," scribbled above my signature.

Either my mother or Brian would help me get gas in one of three different gas cans when I needed it, and that would last me at least a week. It was fun, rewarding, and financially amazing. Every day, I woke up, got everything ready, and then set off for my mowing day. As I added more clients in the neighborhood, I started to get smart and cluster the same cul-de-sacs together, then I'd mow them on the same day. Eventually, I acquired the business of the middle yards between existing customers. With the end units of a townhouse row, plus the middle five, I could make eighty dollars from that row alone. They were sandwiched together, so I could knock them out in one and a half hours, tops. I had become a full-blown entrepreneur, thanks to Brian.

By early June, I was in full swing and business was booming. I had enough money to buy a new Snapper lawn mower and an Echo two-stroke, gasoline-powered, curved weed trimmer to replace the electric one that had fallen into disarray. I bought a fourth, smaller gas can that held gasoline mixed with oil for the weed whacker. With every purchase that made KWELC more efficient, I was able to add more clients. I was up to nearly one hundred fifty homes, with most wanting a mow twice a month. I was grossing over $3,000 monthly while many of my friends were slinging fries at McDonald's for $8 an hour and not even pulling in a grand a month. By the end of summer, I had a small John Deere riding mower, a pull-behind trailer, and numerous other gizmos I used for trimming, edging, blowing, or mulching. On my fifteenth birthday at the end of July, I celebrated by buying more mowing tools and sharpening some mower blades with the extra birthday cash.

Working hard in the Pennsylvania summer heat was rough. It wasn't always fun, and the money didn't always cure the grumbling I may have had on a 95°F day with 85% humidity. It was hard, back-breaking work at times, and as I grew the business, I had choices to make and people to answer to—my customers. The occasional call for an early schedule change became everyone wanting an extra mow just before Independence Day or Labor Day. Scheduling became tough. Any social life I had dwindled, but I sucked it up and toiled on. Brian would tell me a hard day's work built character and that making my own money would teach me to be disciplined.

The scriptures tell us, "Whatever you do, work at it with all your heart, as working for the Lord, not for human masters, since you know that you will receive an inheritance from the Lord as a reward" (Col 3:23-24). Brian and Lynn worked hard, too. He was a young executive in a hard job, selling copiers and supplies on commission. He taught me how to work hard, be the odd man out by doing so, not leaning or taking a break, but to honor the customers, the work, and my business.

Brian and his wife were devout Catholics, and they followed certain, unbending rules. They taught me to be fair, care for people, be a man of honor and integrity, and work hard. He mentored me when I had no mentor. He taught me so much, and he didn't have to. It wasn't his job, his duty, or his responsibility. He saw a kid who needed guidance and reached out to help, leftover dinner re-creations and all.

From the time I was nine years old, I was often alone at

home. My brother was long gone, and my sister had just left for college. My father was rarely present. Who was going to show me sports? Teach me about girls? Learn how to take care of myself?

God provided Brian.

Brian would go on to help me run for student body president during my sophomore year of high school by printing off hundreds of "Vote for Kyle" 11 x 17-inch posters. When he helped me plaster them all over the school at 7:00 a.m. before school opened, everyone assumed he was my dad. I didn't correct them.

Brian and Lynn eventually got pregnant with their first child and moved not too far away into a single-family home. Close, but still a car's drive away. I started seeing him less and less as I got older, and with kids of his own, he poured himself into his boys, as he should have. Eventually, I sought mentorship elsewhere.

Today, when I'm home alone with a mixture of leftovers from the fridge in front of me from the week's prior meals or watching a rerun of *Coach* on TV, it's hard not to wonder where he is today, how much I could bench press in his little weight room as an adult, and how much I owe him for caring for me wildly during a summer of change and into manhood. Brian manifested God to me before I knew what I was missing.

5 | THE CJ-5

"Any man can be a father,
but it takes someone special to be a dad."
—Anne Geddes

My father came to the principal's office, whose secretary called down to my classroom to ask for me to come in. All my teacher said was, "Your father is here to see you." I was petrified. First, I thought I was in trouble and racked my brain as to what I'd done the previous few days. My father—whom I rarely saw, maybe only one weekend a month—was here? In school? My stomach dropped. Was everyone okay? Did somebody die? What did I do that they called my father of all people? My mother and father divorced when I was a toddler and seeing him regularly—least of all in school—was a rarity.

Roland Stanley Duford was a presence of a man if there ever were one. He was six foot five and had hands the size of baseball mitts like old school style Shoeless Joe Jackson-era gloves that were thick, lumpy, and large. He chain-smoked Pall Mall cigarettes, and his gray hair had long ago turned yellow from the plume of tar smoke that constantly enveloped his head. It only made him more mysterious.

He was strong, too. He would use his mass to lift objects not able to be lifted by other men. The time I saw him lift a five-hundred-gallon paint drum into the back of his Ford pickup, my jaw was stuck open for a month. He was also a sight for other reasons. He'd wear nice dress pants with untucked dress shirts that were sleeveless because after buying a pack of them at Men's Warehouse, the kind in cellophane cocoons, he'd remove the pins and hold up the shirt high as if Mufasa were blessing baby Simba. Then he'd grab the collar in one hand and a sleeve in the other and—*POP!*—the sleeve was released like a kid popping a dandelion's head off. He'd then wear this new shirt, unbuttoned as far as it could go while still barely keeping it closed, leaving a mass of gray chest hair with a thick gold chain buried underneath. The chain was a gift from "The Greeks" with whom he played illegal poker for money in the back office of a seedy Allentown bar while I was up front at the bar drinking a Shirley Temple and watching the Philadelphia Eagles play.

That was my father. You didn't mess with him, least of all me. He hit me exactly once, my mother told me, when I had used all her oil paints on top of his brand-new pool table. Apparently, I was two years old. I must remember it subconsciously because I never crossed him again. I saw people who tried, and it wasn't pretty. Now he was in my principal's office, and I was convinced it wasn't going to be pretty for me, either.

I walked into the main office, and Mrs. Jarrell was staring at me as if to say, "What did you do?" I had dated her daughter, Amanda, for a while, so I was friendly with the family, and they had definitely never heard about my father before, so it must've been a shock. I hung my head, and I walked past her and opened the cracked door.

There was the principal, Mr. Tershak, sitting in his chair on the other side of his desk, facing me. My father was to the left, in a chair facing the desk. I kept my hand on the knob and just stood there, poised to run quickly in case things got ugly.

"Hey, Ky," said my father in a friendly voice—I hated when

he called me that. "Come here."

It must've taken me a second to register because he repeated himself. As I walked closer to him, he reached over to the window and spread open a section of blinds between his thick, yellow, cigar-sized index finger and thumb to reveal a jacked-up blue 1984 Jeep CJ-5 sitting directly outside the window, on the sidewalk no less. The black soft top was off, as were the doors, revealing a giant gear shifter on the floor with a heavy knob sitting on top. I salivated. I had seen that Jeep days before as we drove by it in Emmaus, stopping by to inquire on the cost. But in the end, we had driven off. Now it was on the sidewalk of my high school.

"We're going to rebuild it, fix her up, and then it's yours," he said.

"What?" I said. "You're kidding."

"We fix her up, get a new top, and this summer when you turn sixteen, well, she's yours. You can pull a trailer for your lawn business."

She. *Why do guys name their vehicles?* I remember thinking. *What will I call "her?"*

"Ky?" he said. "What are you thinking?"

"I mean, Dad, I love it. Thank you."

"Great, let's go take a look, if that's okay with Mr. Tershak?

"Yeah, yeah, of course. Mind if I go, too?"

"Come on," my father said.

When my mother found out, she made him sell it because she thought it was too dangerous. He didn't have my back on that one, and no one ever brought it up again.

My father ended up married a bunch more times after his marriage to my mother—a bunch being so many that I honestly don't know how many wives he had. I think seven. In between wives, however, man did he love me. When he had someone's attention, though? Well, then he was like, "Kyle who?"

The blue CJ-5 was between wives.

For not being a big car guy, he liked to talk about them and buy them—he just didn't know much about them, especially under the hood. How he would've fixed that Jeep was a mystery. He always paid cash and always had at least two vehicles: a brand-new Cadillac—"The best," he would say—and a Ford F-150 for his business, Duford Painting Company, that painted structural steel and impossible-to-paint buildings and structures, like roller coasters and steel girdings of factories, which was a massive endeavor and a large business to handle.

A few years earlier, at the beginning of summer, while playing in the yard of my mother's house, I heard an interesting sound. The low rumble was something I had never heard before; it got louder and louder before I saw my father whip around the corner in a brand new 1984 Ford Mustang convertible with a 5-liter engine and over 360 horsepower. The body was drastically customized, and the money that was put into that car to make it one of two like it in the world was remarkable. He was there to pick me up for the usual, but occasional, weekend father-son time in his new getup, "The Mouse," as he called it, even though that thing did anything but squeak; it rumbled.

For a while after, if it was a nice day when he'd pick me up, he'd bring "The Mouse." It would be just the two of us in that two-seater, cruising down Hamilton Boulevard on the way to his house, the wind in our hair. Just two guys racing the ponies.

"Dad," I asked when I was about fifteen. "Can I take this car to prom when I'm in high school?"

"Ky, you can *have* it in a few years. This is yours," he said.

"It is?" I questioned.

"Of course, champ. You just have to be careful and do well in school and 'The Mouse' is yours."

Throughout my junior year, I was driving a 1974 Ford F-150 truck with big whitewall tires that got three miles to the gallon, a consolation prize for not getting that CJ-5. The truck was one of my dad's employee's trucks who'd had a heart attack and died, and my dad bought it off the estate for a few hundred dollars. I used it for my business, but I didn't want to take my date in an old truck, so when prom time came, I reminded my father about our deal.

"Hey, Dad," I said when he picked up the phone.

"What's up, Ky?" he rasped back.

"Well, you know my prom is coming up in a few weeks, right?"

"Yeah. . . . Do you need money?" he asked.

"No, no, no," I said. "It's just that . . ."

"Yeah?"

"Well, you know, the Mustang."

"What about it?" he asked.

"Well, you had always said I could take it to prom, and prom is coming up."

"I never said that."

"Uh, you did. Many times. When I turn sixteen and go to prom, you were going to let me have 'The Mouse.'"

"Ky, that doesn't sound familiar. I don't think I would've said that. You know how expensive a car is?"

"Well, yeah, Dad, but—"

"There are only two like them in the world," he said.

I immediately was sullen. "Yeah, Dad, I know. Custom."

"Damn right, custom. The whole thing. Ain't another car like it in the world."

"Well," I said. "One other."

"Smartass," said my father. "Anything else you need?"

Yeah, I need a dad, I thought. But I merely said, "No sir. Goodbye."

He was about to marry wife number six. I was just being a nuisance.

My mother and I had been living in a new home with her long-time boyfriend, Don, who might as well have been my stepfather. He lived with us for over ten years in our previous townhome and well after I went to college. He overheard my conversation with my father and—without asking a soul or telling my mother—got his new white Lincoln Continental detailed and the interior decorated, handed me a hundred-dollar bill, and said, "Go enjoy prom."

A few years later, number six's son turned eighteen. The Mustang was gifted to him for his birthday. Two months later, he wrapped it around a pole while driving home from a party drunk. He was ejected from his seat through the open top, and while flying through the air, had clipped a telephone pole that nearly scalped him. He was in critical condition but survived after a prolonged stay in the intensive care unit. The car, however, was totaled.

For all the men in my life that I learned something from, I learned from him how *not* to be. I had looked up to the man when I was most impressionable, but when things mattered, his superpower was the ability to disappear. It's why I think I always had a hard time believing Jesus would stick around. Oh, he wants to be our Father? Well, he'll probably be the same way because my only example of one was a philandering, narcissistic man who hurt others like it was an Olympic sport.

My father made a lot of promises that fell flat, promises I would remember—and he wouldn't—that never came to fruition. God has never failed on his promises. What a contrast to my father! All through the scriptures, he promises safety, deliverance, protection, love, and so much more, including the big one: eternal salvation with Jesus. God fulfills his Old Testament promises through Jesus, too. I just hadn't experienced that yet. I hadn't found Jesus or my heavenly Father.

Now, being a father myself, it's hard not to fall into the same trap as my father's. I try not to make empty promises, but I'm sure I have. I try to see how Jesus would be to us, how he treated children, and how God the Father wants to love us. It's a stark difference from my father's way and mine, for that matter.

I was disappointed by my father. I think he tried his best, and I eventually forgave him for many of his mistakes. It took me years to learn how to be a dad to my own children, and admittedly, I'm better with the younger ones than the older. I tell my stepdaughter, whose own father isn't involved in her life anymore, "You may not have a father anymore, but you have a dad in me."

When Roland passed away in 2005, I didn't get a chance to tell him that I forgave him, that I was sorry, or that my children were good kids. . . . I was still too hurt, and I even skipped the funeral.

For all the bad memories I had of him, I had many that were good. That Jeep, for one, was his idea. Also, he would take me where I needed to go before I had a car, bought me a nice SLR camera when I was on the school newspaper staff, and spotted me money when I needed it. I wished he was there more, but I see him now as a broken man. I hadn't before.

My Aunt Bonnie, his sister, told me that he finally found peace and love with his last wife, Maggie. She was there with him when he died and was madly devoted to him. After he died, she moved to Israel to the holy land. "He urged me to go," she told me. *What? My dad?* She also told me he had very few things on his desk the day he left the earth: a picture of him and me and a letter I wrote to him in 1997 telling him I was getting married.

6 | CHESS CLUB

"It is sinful to bore kids with the gospel. Christ is the strongest, grandest, most attractive personality to ever grace the earth."
—Jim Rayburn, Founder of Young Life

I can't remember the time or place, but here was this guy: college-aged, driving a baby-blue Volkswagen Rabbit, and hanging around Parkland High School. My school. Odd, for sure, but we would come to find out he was fun. Some of my high school friends were drawn to him immediately for his penchant for breaking into the school's track field to have make-shift decathlons or for driving his little Rabbit onto the local Allentown Municipal Golf Course at midnight. Not into the parking lot, but literally *onto* the course. He had figured out that the width of his little VW was the exact same as the golf cart paths. I can see the nighttime grounds crew now chasing us in their own golf carts, threatening to call the police after these ridiculous kids in a baby-blue car blasting oldies music.

That was Mike.

He had the same look in his eye as those Jewish summer camp counselors at the JCC Day Camp, but he didn't talk about religion in the same way. He actually didn't talk about it all.

He had something, though, and he invested in us. He helped me fill in the gaps of what a teenage boy needed to learn: how to drive a manual transmission, how to apply for college, and how to wrestle. He had been a high school wrestler and knew I struggled on my wrestling team, so he taught me a few moves I had never learned in practice. One time, I pulled out the "Peterson Roll" during a pre-match wrestle-off and pinned a stunned teammate; it felt like I had won the Olympics.

Here I was, this pudgy, gangly kid whom no one noticed, and then suddenly, I had life in me. Mike brought that to me. His love for life was infectious.

As that summer wore down, our shenanigans only ramped up. We blared The Beach Boys' *Greatest Hits* out that little Rabbit's windows and sang songs until our throats hurt on the way to Ocean City, Maryland. By now, my best friend, Alan, had joined us, and the three of us were inseparable. We'd laugh at lyrics about 409 race cars and pretend the Rabbit was a 1963 Thunderbird burning down the strip. That was, until my father took away the T-bird.

My mother thought Mike was a pervert. Kids laughed at us hanging out with a college kid who "didn't even drink!" but we didn't care. He saw us somehow. He listened to us. We confided in him.

One night, I told a lie about something so routine for me that I now forget what it was. He simply listened to my absurd tale, smiled, and nodded. Then he said, "You know, Kyle, I like you for who you are. You don't have to make up stories for me to like you."

I was so embarrassed that I was caught in a lie that I dug in and told him I wasn't lying, that he should *"Fuck off if you don't believe me!"* Then I stormed into my house and began crying. I was exposed, but I knew I was safe at the same time. It was a weird feeling, being accepted despite my failures. I realized I had nothing to prove, but I still felt alone, like I had ruined something in this burgeoning friendship.

A few weeks later and just prior to the school year starting, we decided to play a nine-hole round of golf—for free, of course, because we just drove the VW Rabbit through the parking lot and onto the path like it was our caddy's golf cart. We were trying to beat the light, but none of us being golfers—and only having a pitching wedge and a 3-iron between the three of us—we struggled to have any sort of a game. While the light sank deeper in the summer sky, Mike laughed, seeing the fun in it all. Alan and I got mad. *Why is he laughing? Why are we doing this? The cops are going to come! We're going to be in so much trouble!*

"Why the hell do you even hang out with us?" I screamed, frustrated with life in general and the uncertainty of the upcoming school year. "What's wrong with you? Are you some sort of weirdo?"

There I was, yelling at the top of my lungs at 10:00 p.m. on a Tuesday summer night at some strange man with whom we had just hung out with all summer. My mother had no idea where I was. He could've killed us and buried our bodies on the tenth green—if we could've found it—and no one would've known. But I kept pushing him and pushing him to talk. I wanted answers.

"I think you guys are cool," he said.

"Bullshit!" I yelled in response. "Why. Do. You. Hang. Out. With. Us?"

Mike looked down. A wry little smile took his face. He knew it was time to say something. "Well," he said, "it's because of Jesus Christ."

I had no idea what that meant. I just knew it was religious somehow. "I don't ever want to talk about that again! You keep that to yourself."

"Oh, man, you're missing out. Christ is cool. He's not boring!"

"*Stop*," I snapped back. "No, I don't want religion."

"He's not religious. He's amazing," said Mike.

He went on to say that Jesus was a rebel. He hung out with the truly cool kids, not the cheerleaders and football players, but the bad wrestlers and the liars. He wanted to know the kids who sang Beach Boys songs and not just the kids singing Wilson Phillips or Madonna. He hung out with sinners, and if he were here today, he went on, he'd break into track stadiums and golf courses and hang out with people like us.

I was incensed. I felt duped and sad. "You can hang out with us still," I said, "but not if you talk about this."

Then, after a long pause, I looked at him and said, "You know what? Losers play chess and are in the chess club. If you ever want to talk about this again, you refer to this thing"—I pointed to the ground as if I pointed at the conversation—"as the *chess club*. No more Jesus talk."

A few months later, during the fall semester, Alan, Mike, and I were at the Tilghman 8 AMC movie theater for part of our typical Friday night. After I mowed lawns and Alan finished work, we would grab Red Robin Cokes and fries, followed by a movie at the AMC, then maybe Perkins off Route 22 for a late-night muffin. I loved our Friday night routine. We had logged quite a few. In fact, we had watched all the movies, in order of release: *Die Hard 2*, *Ghost*, *Taking Care of Business*, *Presumed Innocent*, *Navy Seals*. If it was action, comedy, or crime—we saw it.

That night, while we were in line for *Pacific Heights*—still one of my favorite films—starring a creepy Michael Keaton and Matthew Modine, Mike looked up and saw a group of kids he knew and excused himself for a few minutes to say hi. Thinking nothing of it, Alan and I continued to banter until we saw from across the lobby the person he was speaking to: Brian Bell.

Now you should know that at Parkland High School, two sports mattered: wrestling and swimming. Our high school was good at both. The swimmers, however, were special. They were treated like gods in our school because of their physiques and athleticism. They were celebrated more than other schools' football players, and everyone knew it.

Brian Bell was the captain of that swim team and the East Penn Conference's Male Swimmer of the Year. He was a six-foot-something senior with a V-shaped frame who dated the Captain of the girls' team, Alison Silvius, a junior like us. And now he was talking to Mike. We were dumbstruck.

As Mike walked back over, smiling to himself, we just stood there staring at him.

"What?" he said.

"You. Know. Brian. Bell?"

"Well, yeah. I don't just hang out with you two guys."

"Wait," I said, "you hang out with *him*? How do you even know him?"

"Oh," said Mike, "he goes to the chess club."

Alan nudged me with the elbow closest to me and spoke out of the side of his mouth as if to hide his words from everyone in the movie theater lobby but me. "Uh, we're going to chess club."

"Damn right we are," I said.

Mike was one of those guys who imbued the phrase "earn the right to be heard." He was caring and kind, never pushy nor ill-intentioned. The night we went to "Club"—ironically, what Young Life called its high school gatherings—was remarkable. Mike brought us to a neighboring high school's because it was more established than ours, and he wanted to make an impression. So, in typical Mike style, the three of us walked in late, and he pointed to the middle of a room with all its furniture removed and about one hundred fifty kids inside, sitting on the floor. "There," he said. "Let's sit there."

We finagled our way in, stepping over teenagers and trying not to fall on them. We squeezed into the exact middle of the room.

We were surrounded by girls. That must've been his plan. That night, Alan and I were more welcomed to a group than ever before. People—girls, even—asked us our names and told us it was nice to meet us. *Us!*

I didn't pay much attention to the content that night as I was in awe of all those people. I just remember this other leader from their high school standing up after the songs and message to say, "This is Young Life, and we'll be here every Wednesday night through the school year. Don't forget you are all welcome to join us in Florida this winter for a week."

Alan looked at me, and that time, I was ready for his words. We said in unison, "We're going to Florida."

I was slowly being shown through Mike it was possible to be cool and still love Jesus. That Jesus himself was the chief outlaw and probably would be wearing checkerboard Vans and not Tevas if he were alive today. Mike loved wildly. He cared for us like no one ever had. He would've done anything to show me Jesus, and in doing so, he showed me everything.

Do you remember the one who showed you Jesus? Not the one who *told* you about him, but the one who *showed* you? Mike showed me. To me, he was Jesus with skin on, everywhere we went: on the golf course, in his little Rabbit, at the movie theater, and even in "chess club."

7 | THE DECISION

*"I waited patiently for the Lord; He turned to me and heard
my cry. He lifted me out of the slimy pit, out of the mud and mire;
He set my feet on a rock and gave me a firm place to stand."*
—Psalm 40:1-2

I became a believer on Dec 30, 1990, at the base of an old, tall sand
pine tree in Ocklawaha, Florida, at about 9:45 p.m. For years
leading up to that moment, I had been searching for belonging and
meaning. That night, I heard the resurrection story at a Young Life
camp, and the message made sense to me. I committed my life to Jesus Christ. I was sixteen years old.

I had gone to camp in Florida along with my best friend,
Alan. At first, when the speaker that week, Greg, a leader from Buffalo, New York, told us about Jesus, I didn't even listen. Then I heard
about Jesus calling Peter and Andrew, two brothers, fishing with no
luck (Mt 4:18). Greg asked us, "What are you fishing for that isn't
working?" Alan and I snapped looks at each other in terror—did he
know we were frauds?

He went on, "Have you been fishing for girls to fill your

void?" Yes, that didn't work. "Sports?" Yes, that didn't work. "School and studies?" Yes, that didn't work.

How did he know this was us? I thought

It seemed he knew that at this point in life, my high school days were made up of hanging out, going to school, trying to get through three hours of wrestling practice, and then biding my time before I had to go home—many times lingering a few too many hours at a friend's house to avoid the loneliness I would feel when I got to my driveway. My parents had long since divorced, and my mother, whom I still lived with, focused solely on herself. My mother's longtime boyfriend, Don, was nice enough and always there but would come home drunk nightly after playing golf. My much-older siblings were still away at college, so I was often lonely at home. I wasn't a "bad" kid. I didn't smoke or drink or run around with girls. I was a typical high schooler, but perhaps unlike my friends who filled their lives with those risky trappings, I was painfully aware of my loneliness.

So naturally, this fisherman business piqued my interest. I wanted the answers, but Greg's talk ended without a resolution. I would have to wait two more days to hear the Good News. That wait didn't suit me. For the next twenty-four hours until the next talk, I had inner turmoil. I knew I wanted something, and somehow it seemed like this Jesus cat could have the answers. But I needed to know more. Could I be a fisher of men, too? Whatever the heck that meant.

The next night was the "cross talk," when we heard about how Jesus had been crucified and that he had died for our sins. I was so saddened by his death. I had not only never heard this story, but I also didn't understand. I thought, *This is good news?* I was so distraught that night that I asked my Young Life leader, Mike, why he'd bring me to this place only to point out my failures, then tell me that the one man who could help me had ended up dead. I felt like the disciples—lost, lonely, and baffled—in the days after his death, hiding in the upper room.

I pressed him, "Please tell me what happened!"

"Let's just wait until tomorrow. But I promise it's good."

The next day I was fraught with fear, doubt, and self-reflection. I hardly enjoyed myself that day at camp with my mind swirling. While nearly everyone else was having the time of their lives, I was counting down the hours to "Club," the nightly get-together of all the high schoolers and their leaders. Then I waited as we sang through the Young Life staples of "Barbara Ann," "My Girl," and "40" by U2.

"Why are we singing U2?" I asked.

"We're not just singing U2," said our leader. "U2 is singing the Bible."

Finally, Greg came up, and he resumed the story from the night before. I was rapt with attention.

After he finished with the empty tomb, we had a moment of silence when the kids left the club room to find a spot to ourselves to reflect on the message. If we wanted to, we could pray to God and use the "A-B-Cs": Accept Jesus was Lord, Believe in his resurrection, and Commit our life to him . . . at the base of that old sand pine tree.

After some time had passed, we all returned to the clubhouse. Greg recapped and suggested that if we had made a decision that night, we should tell our friends and leader during cabin time.

"Well, guys," said Mike back in the cabin. "Anyone decide to follow Jesus tonight?"

A few of us raised our hands sheepishly, not knowing who else had or hadn't.

"I did," I finally said.

"Tell us about that."

"Well, it just made sense to me," I said. "I think I always felt something was out there. I guess it was . . . God?"

I thought something would happen to me, like I would have

felt a transformation. *If the Holy Spirit would be in my life, wouldn't I feel Him?* I wasn't even twenty-four hours or so into my new life to follow Christ, but I was so new in my faith—extremely green and wet behind the ears.

"What will change?" I asked my leader.

"Well," he said, "the Bible says that if anyone is in Christ, he is a new creation," and then shared his J.B. Phillips version of the New Testament with me:

> This means that our knowledge of men can no longer be based on their outward lives (indeed, even though we knew Christ as a man, we do not know him like that any longer). For if a man is in Christ, he becomes a new person altogether—the past is finished and gone, everything has become fresh and new. All this is God's doing, for he has reconciled us to himself through Jesus Christ, and he has made us agents of the reconciliation. God was in Christ personally reconciling the world to himself—not counting their sins against them—and has commissioned us with the message of reconciliation. We are now Christ's ambassadors, as though God were appealing directly to you through us (2 Cor 5:17-21).

"Okay," I said. "I think this makes sense. What do I do now?"

"Well, I'm going to get you a Bible you can have. I encourage you to start reading it. Start with The Gospel of Matthew and try to read at least a chapter a day. Then I want you to start coming to Campaigners."

"What's that?"

"It's like Club, but everyone who comes has made a decision like you did at some point."

"Oh, okay. I guess I'll come, too."

While that night had changed my life, assuredly, I was ill-equipped to understand what it meant to be a new Christian. I would move toward the side of legality and outward proclamation rather than understanding the Holy Spirit in me and who God wanted me to be.

That decision started the legalism in my mind, though I didn't know that was what it was yet. My heart made the decision about Jesus, but I started immediately following the rules: Go to Campaigners, read my Bible, learn how to pray, don't be bad, respect my mom, be on time.

This rule-following didn't make as much sense as the gospel did. But I figured, to belong in this new world, it was time to be someone I wasn't. I pulled on a mask.

8 | DEVIL'S SLIDE

"Through him, all things were made; without him, nothing was made that has been made."
—John 1:3

Rock climbing for the first time was scary, and when I virginly rappelled down a wall, I was petrified. Over time, though, the skills I developed—and my finger and forearm strength—served not only to heighten my ability but also make the experience more fun. I was ready to go outside.

Craig, Brian the Xerox man's brother-in-law, was a local who loved to climb, too. He was a skilled photographer with longer hair, a cool vibe, and flannel shirts worn months before Nirvana and Pearl Jam made it popular. He drove a Jeep Wrangler Sahara, green body with a tan soft-top, and exuded "cool" from all his pores. His wife, Laurie, was Lynn's, Brian's wife's sister, and the four of them would often gather in our neighborhood, walking Brian's dog with him. On the days I joined, I slowly got to know Craig and thought to myself, *This is who I want to be when I grow up.* When he learned I was climbing inside, he offered to take me outside on real rock.

Like his brother-in-law, Craig cared for me. He'd pick me up on Saturday mornings, or I'd meet him in Philly at the rock and go for a few hours of fun. We'd talk about marriage, how he met his wife—whom I'd had a big crush on since I was fourteen—what it was like to be married, and the struggles they had as a couple.

Craig showed me that you can still be doing fun, amazing things in life without sacrificing anything else, but I could tell he also longed for something I was never able to put my finger on. I suspected on some level he needed a partner, and I was that lucky little fella. Like a Robin to his Batman, he could call on me with a moment's notice and I'd be there, ready for him. I was his climbing partner and his confidant, and for years, he was the only person I would ever allow to belay me—being my safety partner. Similarly, he trusted a seventeen-year-old boy to hold his secrets, his struggles, and his heart.

He was such a good artist and photographer. I envied his ability, so I ended up enrolling in Craig's alma matter at Kutztown University when the prospect of paying for my number one choice, Hofstra University, was untenable. Soon after I enrolled, Craig ended up getting divorced. He packed up his life and headed to Colorado, where the climbing was epic.

I was so jealous, but I would be right behind him.

As soon as I started my first year of college, I knew I didn't want to go back home to my mother when it was over, so by December of 1992, I had already applied everywhere I could in the hope of getting a job locally. Nothing really solidified, but while ending my freshman year's first semester at KU, I was perusing my copy of *Climbing* and saw an advertisement in the classifieds for a climbing instructor.

Looking for Mountaineer

Intervarsity Christian Fellowship's Bear Trap Ranch in Colorado Springs, Colorado, is looking for a gifted and

skilled climbing instructor to lead college groups this summer. Apply with resume and letter to Bear Trap Ranch, 8655
Old Stage Rd, Colorado Springs, CO 80906.

I applied for the position, even though I wasn't really suited
for it. That was before the internet and email, so I typed a letter, got
references, and dropped off the letter at the local Kutztown post office, which still had rails outside for the Amish to tie up their horses
and buggies. I held my breath.

After about four weeks, I received a phone call. Actually, my
roommates received the call and failed to give it to me, but eventually, I received an obscure piece of paper with instructions to call
back the camp director, Mark. When we finally spoke, he said they'd
love to set up an interview with me to see if I would like to join them
for the summer. Of course! I thought. So without hesitation, we set
up a time for an interview a few days later. During the interview, I
continued to espouse my unbelievable rock climbing skills, which
didn't actually exist. I gave two references, my youth group leader
and my high school ex-girlfriend's mom—she had always thought I
needed "more Jesus in my life," and a summer in the mountains with
him would be perfect.

A few weeks later, I got the news: I was in. Two of us were
chosen from about a hundred applicants across the country, and
when we arrived, they'd decide who'd be the head mountaineer and
who would be the assistant.

I only had one year of school under me, and that school was
without an Intervarsity chapter, so I had no idea what I was getting
myself into. I had thought that Intervarsity was basically Young Life
for college, but I couldn't have been more wrong. All the shenanigans
I had gotten into in high school in Young Life flew under the guise
of "Jesus is fun." Now that same reckless abandon of faith was not
welcome as an eighteen-year-old with two semesters of English lit-

erature courses under his belt. I was expected to be more adult-like, but I was just a kid in a slightly older form. I often got myself into trouble by telling a few off-color jokes or hitting on too many college girls from midwestern schools. I was in full-on summer Beach Boys mode, and last I had heard, the Midwest farmers' daughters really helped you feel all right, so I tried to date a few, but Intervarsity didn't see the humor in that.

I also thought I was hot shit. Anything anyone else did, I felt like I could do better, but in reality, I was in a new world: in my faith, with new colleagues and peers, and now in the Rocky Mountains, living at 8,500 feet above sea level in an atmosphere that was far above even the highest rock climbs in Pennsylvania. I was slow to discover that the same defense mechanisms I held aloft in high school were following me into this new situation, my first time west of Pittsburgh.

The first three weeks of camp were pretty much cleaning the trails, inspecting the ropes, testing out the harnesses, and learning to trust each other. I met my partner on the first day, Adam from New Jersey, where it's just as flat, if not more so, as where I grew up outside Philly. He was my height, my age, but better in every way. Adam was confident and Christlike. He was humble, soft-spoken, his face an olive complexion that was not only smooth but never had seen a razor. He was the all-American boy next door. He was also a little uptight and churchy, but he grounded my behavior. If I was the loose cannon Maverick, he was Goose. But Adam had never seen *Top Gun*—he wasn't allowed—so he never understood the reference.

Within the first week, I was named the head mountaineer and Adam the assistant, even though he had much more skill than I did, even being from Jersey. Routes—the particular path you climb—are graded into a difficulty scale from 5.0 to 5.15. Typically, anything below 5.7 is considered easy, scalable, maybe without any rope. 5.8 to 5.10 is considered intermediate, 5.11 to 5.12 is hard, and anything over 5.13 is reserved for the few elite climbers. I was climbing 5.10s while Adam was climbing at least 5.11s and much more gracefully. I took this "leadership" role not as seriously as I should have, but I did, in fact, use it to beef up my ego even more.

Behind one of the tiny cabins used for the climbing equipment was a small spire of rock, long-ago bolted for sport climbing that had tethers at the very top for easy top-roping. You could do a somewhat easy climb/walk up the back to the top of the spire to drop ropes and get the day ready for the students to climb.

Top-roping is basically when the rope goes from the ground—attached to you—up to the very top of the climb—usually through some carabiners—and then back down to the bottom, attached to a belayer's harness via a belay device, which is used to stop any misstep from being a disaster. As long as you were accurately secured, falling off the wall would merely lead to a big swing and bungee-like give in the rope, or maybe a wedgie in the process.

One day, as I traversed too far to the right while practicing, I slipped and "took a whipper" off the wall. Although not falling *down*, I swung *across*. Along the way, I snapped a pine sapling in half, and then on the return swing, the snapped trunk sliced through my T-shirt and skin all in one fell swoop. I still have a four-inch scar on my mid-back from that day.

It's not nearly as dangerous as lead-climbing, where the rope runs directly from your belay partner to you, the climber. As you ascend the rock, you "clip" the rope into bolts or other forms of gear that are either fixed to the rock or inserted into it. If you fall here, you fall twice the distance from your last piece of gear to you, which is why you typically want to place your protection every five to six feet, so your maximum fall isn't more than a simple twelve-foot drop. We weren't teaching lead climbing that summer, just top-rope climbing. And that was a good thing because I had never led a climb.

A few days prior to our arrival, a camp cook arrived on site to get the kitchen ready. His name was Erik. Erik, although our cook for the summer, was an experienced climber from Colorado and had much more experience climbing the granite rock formations that were very common in the Rockies, especially at this altitude. He wore glasses and always a dirty, old, faded ball cap turned backward so as not to get in the way of either the cooktop vent or the rock he was climbing. He had applied three summers consecutively for the mountaineering positions, each year being denied but offered a slot in the kitchen, where he would often regale stories about climbing routes in and around the mountains off of Cheyenne Canyon to which Adam and I would both roll our eyes, thinking we were much better than him because we had the title—and he didn't.

The last week before family camp started, we had one or two days where the full camp staff of about twenty-two college students and three or four full-time staff got together to do trust building, involving some sort of climbing or horseback riding activity. At the end of the day, the adult staff leader invited Adam and me to his cabin for dinner, where he and his wife were entertaining his old college friends from Baylor University, Dave and Patti Bechtold, who had come up from their home in the Springs. At the end of a long, exhausting staff day, it was fun to talk about life, hobbies, and the wonders of Colorado. Dave and I talked briefly about where we were from and how much I enjoyed Colorado.

Adam and I were invited to stay and watch the *Cheers* finale on a television set so old its reception was from an old set of rabbit ears. In the time leading up to it, and between commercials, Dave peppered us with questions about what we aspired to be one day and how we were enjoying the summer. I told Dave how my time in Colorado was an escape from home and that while I was still searching for meaning and belonging, something in Colorado was calling my name. When the show was over, he and his family went back down the mountain.

For the most part, this was our life in the mountains—climbing, eating, fellowship, and new people—and I thoroughly enjoyed it. There was something about waking up in the crisp and cool air of Colorado in late May at a high-altitude camp only to drink cowboy coffee and spend time with kids my age who believed in the same God who had created it all. The days started with that crisp coldness but would warm up as it went along. Sometimes it might even snow at night, but it was just perfect, nonetheless. That clean air I had never felt before in my lungs. It was absolutely home. It was especially epic waking up in an old cabin, where Adam and I shared a room heated by a single gas wall burner, only to go outside into all that wonder. I loved sharing a room with a guy as kind as Adam, even though he didn't like the fact that I played the Red Hot Chili Peppers on my stereo. That was "the Devil's music."

On our first full day off in twenty days, Adam and I decided to climb the big tower that rose far above camp and would cast a shadow on us for an hour during the day. This unnamed tower was sitting atop "Devil's Slide," a large round mass of rock just off the western side of the long and winding dirt Gold Camp Road. For some reason, we didn't quite prepare, and I was in jeans rather than my climbing pants, and Adam wasn't feeling so good, but we went on anyway. The plan was to hike the forty-five-minute trail up to the base of the Slide, then another thirty or so minutes to get to the top of the rock where the base of the tower started.

As we were hiking out of camp, Erik looked out the back door of the kitchen and asked if he could join. Uninterested in his company, I quipped, "Sure, but we're not waiting for you. If you can catch up, you can join us."

Fifteen minutes later, we heard the clanking of Erik's sling with his gear slapping each other as he ran up to us. "Hey, guys. Thanks!" We rolled our eyes.

When we got to the base of the climb, I was nervous. The

only way to climb this tower was to lead it. And although I had the gear, I didn't have the ability, and more significantly, I had never led a lead climb. Without hesitation, however, I decided to go first— though I never gave anyone else a chance to want to.

While Adam went around to a tree to urinate, Erik and I rigged up and set off. The rock was dusty and dirty, and I couldn't hold a grip, but that didn't deter me the way it should have. At five feet, I added some gear into the wall to secure me. Anxious and shaking, I kept going. Ten feet. Fifteen feet. Twenty feet. I was climbing well above my ability on dirty rock that, to our knowledge, had never been climbed before, let alone by a kid who had never led a route in his life nor climbed anything above fifty feet outside Philadelphia.

Then the holds went sparse. The rock got solid. The only crack in which to place my hands was in the corner of the dihedral. I wedged my fingers in there for dear life, pulling my body away from the wall in a "layback," where my weight pulling away was giving me the grip I needed.

In that position, I looked up and saw a large ledge that could've held a Mack truck. *If I can only get there, I can relax*, I thought. So I motored on.

I had a choice to make: hold myself in place and then keep moving with both my hands or try to add more protection into the rock to ensure my safety. The problem was, climbing above my grade, I was unable to hold myself up one-handed so I could reach for a piece of gear. I knew the farther I climbed, the more danger I was in, but I had no choice.

When I made the ledge—roughly forty-five feet up—I was well past my safety gear. I had "run out" the rope, so if I were to fall, I'd hit the ground, having more rope above my last anchor than below it. That was all I could think about, and when I reached for my gear, that was exactly what happened. I fell the entire distance and hit the ground.

At the base of the rock was a larger triangle-shaped boulder the size of a small house. It had fallen off the top years ago and landed exactly at the base, so if you wanted to climb the spire, you first had to scramble up this piece of rock on its 45° angle face, which made it easy to reach the start of the climb.

My feet hit this large boulder first, but because it was on such an angle, I immediately started falling backward from there, in a sort of reverse somersault, end-over-end for what must have been a dozen flips. Each time I came around, I hit the rock harder as my speed increased. When I came to rest, I had broken thirteen bones, shattered my left forearm, and smashed the back left side of my skull.

Thank God Erik was there—he was the only one who knew wilderness medicine. Adam ran for help.

June 4, 1993, was not a good day for me.

When I later woke up in Memorial Hospital, crowds of students, doctors, and nurses were around me. No one knew if I'd wake up at all due to the three hematomas on my brain. My arm wasn't even fixed, just strapped down so as to not injure it further. A tube ran from my head to a small bag clipped to my hospital gown. My head was shaved, cut open, reconstructed, and stapled back up. Blood was caked onto my torso and face. They asked me a few questions, which I answered satisfactorily, I must imagine, because there was a mild cheering from the crowd of nurses and medical students. They then increased some fluid into my IV, and I fell back to sleep on the drugs.

Later that day, I started to hear the beating of my heart rate, steady on a machine in my room. Electronic and steady, it was the only noise I heard. I was lying on my right side, as all the damage was on the left side of my body—arm, head, collar bone, and ribs. I had a pillow stuffed behind my back so I wouldn't roll over. I slowly opened my swollen eyes in the recovery room. The light was dim but not off, and the shades were semi-drawn to let in some light but not wake me. I blinked a few times. It wasn't a dream. I was there. And I was alive.

Near the foot of the bed, but just to the left of it, back against the wall where the television hung, was a man sitting in a chair. I had to squint to see him, as my vision was still a bit blurry and my head throbbing with pain. It was Dave, the guy from our dinner a week or two before.

"Hey, man," he said. "I came as soon as I heard the news."

"Dave . . . ?"

"Yeah, it's me. I just knew you didn't have family here and wanted to make sure someone was here when you woke up."

"How long have you been here?" I asked.

"I don't know, a couple of hours or so," he said. On his lap in front of him, he held a stack of books, like he was checking out of a library. "I brought you a bunch of books to read. I'm not sure what you like, so here are several."

He started to read them aloud: "*This Present Darkness, The Firm, Patriot Games*—ooh, I think another one of his is coming out soon. I brought you some of my girl's Dr. Suess books, a *TIME* magazine, and today's newspaper."

"Thanks, Dave. That's very kind of you," I said softly.

"You're welcome. I'm happy to read one to you if you want."

"Thanks. Maybe not now, but thank you," I said.

"You gave us quite a scare, Kyle. You're lucky to be alive," said Dave, his head hung low to hide tears welling up in his eyes. "We've all been praying for you."

"Alive?" I said. "What happened? I was climbing with Adam—or Erik, or—"

"I'm sure the guys can fill you in. All I know is that it was a long rescue—ten hours or so—to get you off that cliff. The helicopter couldn't land, so they brought you down in an ambulance after they rappelled you off the rock."

I had no idea what he was talking about.

At that moment, two of the last people I wanted to see—or imagined seeing—walked into the room—together. My father and mother came in.

Crying, my mother ran to my right bedside, pushing Dave slightly out of the way. "Honey," she said, "we're so happy you're okay."

Clearly, I was anything but.

"Hey, champ," said my father. "Any cute nurses giving you a sponge bath?"

"Roland!" my mother snapped back. "Stop it."

They hadn't been in the same room in nearly twenty-five years, and now they had not only flown out together on the same plane but were in my room—together.

By the time I knew what was happening, I noticed that Dave had quietly slipped out, leaving the books on the chair he had occupied and my two parents arguing in front of my bed.

Just like that, he was gone.

The days that followed are a blur. Once my father realized I would be okay and that his chances of scoring a nurse for himself were slim, he hopped a flight back to Pennsylvania. My mother stayed a few days to see how I was healing. Then the doctors gave me the news.

"I'm afraid your hemoglobin and hematocrit levels are too low, son," said the doctor. "Unless your H and H levels improve, there's no way you can go back to that elevation; you don't have enough oxygenated blood cells."

"But . . . I want to go back to the camp," I said.

"I'm afraid that's out of the question. It's hard enough here in

Colorado Springs at this elevation. I can't let you go back to 9,500 feet."

"That's okay, honey," said my mother. "You can come home with me and heal up."

That was not going to happen. I had spent my teenage years trying to leave town. I couldn't imagine being in a bed in my mother's house, unable to move or do much, and have her in my face, wondering why I hadn't gotten up for the day.

"When does it need to be back to normal?" I asked.

"You'll be discharged in a few days," he said. "Let's check again then. If they're not back to normal, we can discuss options."

Great! Options, that was one thing I didn't have.

Dave would appear at random times during my short hospital stay, and there was never a day he didn't come by. I'm not sure how he did it with a busy household full of children, but he managed, nevertheless, and I looked forward to his stay. We'd talk about the books he had brought—I had devoured *This Present Darkness* and asked for its sequel—what I was watching on television, and anything *but* my injury. On one of his visits, my mother must've been out for a walk because he caught me alone.

"Oh, they set your arm?" he said excitedly.

"Yeah, yesterday, finally."

"Green cast?" he asked, looking at my Hulk-green-colored forearm.

"I figured in the mountains, it'd blend in when I go back to camp," I replied. "I didn't think it'd be so . . . neon."

We both laughed until my laughter turned to tears.

"Kyle, what's wrong?" he asked.

I told Dave about my trouble with my blood levels. The subsequent results weren't high enough to release me to the camp, but they were going to discharge me from the hospital anyway. I'd have to go back home.

"Hey, hey, hey," he said, "it'll be okay."

"I can't go back home, Dave. It's awful. My mom moved with her boyfriend to a farm in the middle of nowhere. All my friends are in college. I just . . . can't go back."

"Kyle, you don't have to, man."

"Dave, you're not listening to me—I have no choice."

Then he just looked at me, his mustache up-turned by his smile. "You can stay with us."

"What?" I said.

"Patti and I spoke the other day in case this happened. We have a full basement apartment, with a full bathroom and television. You can stay there as long as you need to."

"But I have doctors' appointments and your kids, and—"

"Kyle," he interrupted me, "let us do this for you."

My mother reluctantly went home after I got situated at the Bechtold's, and I spent nearly four weeks at Dave's house, recovering from my injuries. I bled through many of his pillows and slept through dinners. Nothing phased them. They took me to the neurosurgeon to get my massive staples removed from my head and helped me get my arm recast. They even helped me shower and shave. They wanted to show their love by serving me in my incapacitated state. When my levels increased enough to return to camp—although not as a mountaineer, but as the head of the dishwashing crew—they even drove me up and hugged me goodbye.

I have never met anyone like Dave and his family. I likely never will. We rarely spoke about Jesus or what they worshipped; he never told me how to think and behave. Their actions said everything. They exuded Jesus from every pore. They loved me, took me in, fed me, and literally clothed me when I couldn't do it for myself. Dave and his wife were a combination of both the Good Samaritan and the friends who brought their paralyzed friend to Jesus. Nothing would stop them from helping me heal, both physically and emotionally, from my bruises back home.

Dave had met me exactly once, over a pot of spaghetti while visiting his college friends. And that changed everything.

9 | THE BADMINTON COURT
"I'm gonna soak up the sun.
I'm gonna tell everyone to lighten up."
—Cheryl Crow, "Soak up the Sun"

It was a beautiful June in Boulder in the summer of 1996—crisp nights and warm days rarely reaching above 90°F. With not too much heat in the forecast, the students who decided to stay back in town were fired up for summer, enjoying what the town had to offer. I was one of them. I lived in a summer sublet in a room of a Young Life house with some friends of mine. Some of them had lived there for years and had a ritual down for the summer. So I joined the madness while I took a few classes to get ahead.

There were four of us, including Frank, who had lived there nearly all four years of college at CU-Boulder. Frank was one of those guys you just had to see to believe existed. He looked and dressed like Alex P. Keaton from *Family Ties* and—like his 1980s television show doppelgänger—was also a staunch Republican. I could imagine him wearing a tie every day in high school or carrying a briefcase through the lunch hall. During his college days, he drove an old

Chrysler K-car that we would tease him about because it looked like an old FBI car, which we truly thought he was secretly one of. We weren't joking.

Frank had never lost his swimming physique from high school, even if he was losing some of his raggedy yet carefully positioned blond hair. He was my age, twenty-two, but unlike me, he had already graduated from the university the month prior. Even before graduation day, he had scored what he called his dream job, working for a secret contractor of the United States State Department forty-five minutes away in Aurora, Colorado.

"Until I get my security clearance," he told us, "I don't have much to do." They set him up with a computer with two games: golf and solitaire. The first six months were spent getting paid for walking into a very large lobby, greeting the receptionist, and then going into another large room with twenty cubicles full of other people like him, stuck in their own security clearance, golf-playing limbo. To get past the next level of security, we wondered if he needed FBI clearance or just a high score in solitaire.

When he eventually got his clearance, everything was a secret. All we ever knew was that he would leave in the morning, come back at night, and never tell us a thing. Because he had his degree in aerospace engineering, we knew the job he was doing was with military contracts, or at least we pretended it was. He'd come home, and we would say something like, "How was your day designing Maverick missiles?" Or "How is the new stealth bomber?" Once when he had led a team on a successful project, the plaque in which he was presented could've been in hieroglyphs and been clearer: "To Frank, for that thing you did, on that important project, and for leading some people on X4-7384."

But before his clearance, he was bored at work, and I was bored taking three summer semester classes, so we decided to make the nights more interesting. *What else is more interesting than playing badminton in the backyard?* we all thought. The four of us would play each night, under the lights and under pseudonyms. I was the one from Scotland, and Frank was called Bridger Sterling, a "badminton extraordinaire and taunting, self-absorbed ass," in his words. When he was the referee, he played Xiao Wang, the corrupt and contemptuous, unfair linesman from China. The other two guys would randomly change characters from places like Paraguay, Germany, Spain, or Australia, depending on their mood.

One night after about nine o'clock—and probably after having a few too many beers—we sat, looking at this sad, sloppy backyard court. "We know!" we said. "Let's create a Wimbledon-style proper badminton court!" We thought that made perfect sense. That meant we needed to level the grass, cut it very short, and make it work somehow. The yard in the back was not quite level, so first thing first: we had to mow it down and see what we had. After a single mow, we realized the soil underneath was so uneven that the next thing that needed to happen was to—naturally—dig up the backyard and plant new grass.

Though the process was daunting, we aerated the entire lawn, ripped up the square patch underneath what would be our future beautiful world championship court, and either laid down new dirt and tamped it down flat or planted new seeds. We then watered this area every night for about six hours for at least five weeks. We hadn't foreseen that to complete this entire process, we would lose not only our entire summer but also the ability to do anything in the backyard for a while. We also didn't account for all of the water usage. Our landlord would soon reach out to us to see if we had a toilet broken and running because, for "some reason, the water bill was really high."

Each day I looked outside to see if the seedlings on the new turf had sprouted a little bit of green fuzz, and I'd call Frank to report the details while he was sitting in front of a digital tee, wondering which iron to use on today's virtual course.

About halfway through the summer, we saw progress. Over-night, all of the seedlings cracked and started sprouting. I called Frank at the office immediately.

"Hello?" he said.

"Frank! We. Have. Grass!"

"No way! Where?"

"Everywhere," I said. "The entire lawn is sprouting. I'm go-ing to keep watering it."

That night we sat on our cement deck, the four of us, with warm cans of Barq's root beer and a few too many Totino's party piz-zas from the microwave. We celebrated our new achievement.

Each week that would continue. I'd come back from class, see the lawn, and report it to Frank. Of course, he could have easily looked in the morning before he went to work and me before school, but we liked it this way. In some fashion, we were all cultivating a new life on that badminton court for us to play, a metaphor for our changing lives. Checking in was our daily ritual that made the frivolous yard feel more like our ever-changing lives. That went on through the rest of July and most of August. Finally, it was ready to mow and to cut in our court. We fired up the lawnmower, cut the entire lawn, then lowered the mower setting and cut a large area around the court. Then we lowered it some more and cut in the play-ing area. That night, we hung floodlights, practiced our ridiculous accents, and played exactly four games of badminton.

We had spent so long building up something that could've been more fun had we started playing two months earlier. But we were tired of talking about the backyard and just happy the lawn was back to normal and our landlord was done searching the crawl-space for pipe leaks.

The fall semester started inching closer, and we all started getting ready for it. I needed to move out to give back my summer sublet, and Frank ended up getting his clearance a bit earlier than he had originally thought—a great disappointment to us who thought it would be funny to continue our accents when the FBI called to do a reference check on him. (*"'Ello, guvnah, old Frank is at the pub, swilling some pints of ale, mate."*)

The badminton court eventually grew back to a normal lawn, and as the weeks ticked by during the school year, the sag in the net got deeper and deeper until the first snowfall forced the guys to remove it entirely. We had long forgotten why we had originally created the court in the first place. We were so excited about the process that we lost sight of the prize, the outcome. We lost our summer of fun and what we were excited about for daily drudgery. In the end, it wasn't worth it.

When I became a Christian, I had been so involved with the details: having the requisite quiet times with God, reading (and memorizing) scriptures, following the rules, and probably the most egregious, changing who I was. I ripped up my own lawn, sloppy and sad, to plant something new—something I wasn't. But God just wanted to play badminton with me. He wanted to play right then when I had met him years earlier under that tree in Florida, not in the future after I had altered the ground. Right then.

He likes it when we come to him dirty and broken, but I felt like I needed to be perfect. Like the days following my decision to follow him, I thought it all had to be perfect to even play on his court: a quiet time each day, prayer a certain way, church on Sunday, date the perfect girl, and look and talk the same way as other Christians. In the effort it took to get it right, however, I lost interest in playing on his field entirely. It just felt like it took too long.

10 | JERUSHAH

"Let me not to the marriage of true minds
Admit impediments. Love is not love
Which alters when it alteration finds,
Or bends with the remover to remove.
O no, it is an ever-fixèd mark."
—Shakespeare, *Sonnet 116*

By January 1997, I had been back into the normal swing of things: a full class load, trying to learn all about literature and film and all the studies that interested me: History of the Roman Empire, Creative Writing II, and more. I would work locally, cleaning up construction sites on Tuesdays and Thursdays, so I loaded my schedule with all M-W-F classes. Often, I'd park myself for a coffee in University Memorial Center, the hub of the campus itself, before my last class of the day.

The UMC holds the bookstore, some administrative offices, the Panhellenic and Greek offices, and numerous food halls, including the ironically named Alfred Packer Grill, named eponymously after the wilderness guide who infamously killed and ate his fellow travel companions.

Thousands of students and staff pass through the main hallways and seating areas each day, maybe twice, sometimes for a quick bite—sometimes for a chat with friends.

I was sitting with another non-traditional student with whom I had become friends. As we talked about nonsense and music—he was a big fan—I glanced at the table next to me and saw the most beautiful girl I'd ever seen—before or since—sitting with a friend. Shorter, curly hair, with green eyes and a beautiful smile. She had an adorable birthmark just above the left side of her mouth and her smile, when she smiled, won me over.

I tried to catch her eye a few times, and the time we locked eyes for a moment, I knew I wanted to know her. Heck, I thought I would *marry* her.

"Hey, Carlos," I said. "Look at those girls over there."

"Yeah, I noticed," he replied. "Pretty cute," he said as he was looking at the other girl sitting next to her.

"Man, she's amazing," I said, staring at the adorable one.

Just then, they both looked at us, stood up, and started walking toward our table.

"Dude, they're coming over," I said. And before he could even reply, they were standing next to us, looking down at our table.

"Hi," they said. "What are you guys talking about?"

"Not much," I said. "Carlos here was just talking about Stevie Ray Vaughan."

"Who?" said the other girl.

"Stevie Ray Vaughan," said Carlos, annoyed. "Best guitarist ever? Died in a plane crash?"

"Never heard of him," she said.

That whole time, I was just staring at the cute one. "I'm Kyle," I said. "This is Carlos."

"Hi," said the one who didn't know who Stevie Ray Vaughn was. "I'm Olivia. This is my friend, Jerushah."

Ahh, Jerushah. I loved hearing that. *Jerushah*. What a name. "Hi, Jerushah," I said and shook her hand. Then I said her name in my head a few times over: *Jerushah, Jerushah, Jerushah*. I wanted her to say it herself.

"Hi," she blushed. She didn't say her name, but we quickly shook hands and smiled at each other.

"What was your name again?" I said.

"Jerushah."

"Ahh," my smile definitely widened. "I like that."

"Thank you," said Jerushah.

"So what do you guys like to do besides talk about obscure rockstars?" said Olivia.

"He's not obscure," Carlos sighed. "But you know, we hang out, love coffee, I'm pretty busy with school."

"Ahh. Sounds good," she said.

"We wanted to talk to you guys about Jesus," said Olivia.

Carlos rolled his eyes. "No thanks."

"Why not?" asked Jerushah.

"Do you want to discuss the ontological proof for the existence of God?" he said.

"Oh, Aquinas?" said Olivia, stunning Carlos.

"Yeah," he said.

The two bantered at each other for a while in a way that didn't interest me. I caught myself just staring at Jerushah, who was still smiling, looking at me in return.

She gave me a look as if to say, "What about you?" So I preemptively said, "Oh, I play for the same team. I know Jesus. I want to know more about you."

"What do you want to know?" she asked.

"I don't know. Tell me about yourself."

"Well," she said, "Olivia and I have been best friends literally since we were six months old. We moved out here together."

"What are you studying?"

"Well, I don't go here. I go to Ravencrest."

"What is that?" I said.

"It's a Bible school in Estes Park. We're both in a year-long program."

"Oh. So you're down here to . . ."

"Tell people about the Lord. Yeah, it's a little weird, but we had a choice of what to do for an elective, and we figured it'd get us down to Boulder once a week."

"Once a week?"

"We come every Wednesday afternoon."

"How's that going?"

"Well, you're the first two we've talked to." She smiled.

"Oh, well, I'm glad you came over. I noticed you earlier."

"I saw you, too," she said.

There's that smile again, I thought.

She told me more about her. How she had grown up in a typical God-fearing Southern home. She was the granddaughter of Billy Graham, a man who history has now confirmed had spoken in person to more people on Planet Earth than any other living soul, estimated at over 2.2 billion. He was knighted, named one of *TIME* magazine's "100 Persons of the Century" for his influence, set a record for the number of times he adorned the Gallup Poll's Top 10 Most Admired of the Year List with sixty-one mentions, and met with every US President from Eisenhower to Trump. Jerushah's mother was Graham's eldest child of five, and Jerushah herself was the penultimate of seven children. Her parents called her Jerushah after Julie Andrews's character in the 1966 movie *Hawaii*, although later they'd come to find it also appears in the Bible three times.

After a while, they excused themselves as they had to catch the van back to campus. I was too nervous to say anything more to her, so I watched her leave the UMC with her friend, the two of them giggling and smiling the whole way down the hall. I watched them the entire way.

At the very last moment, she turned around to see me, smiled, and then left.

I should've chased after her to ask for her number, but I was too nervous. For seven days, I anxiously waited until the next Wednesday. I couldn't think straight. I couldn't focus. All I wanted to do was to see her again.

When Wednesday came, I parked myself at the UMC all day until she walked in. I asked her out for Saturday, and she said yes, only if I picked her up. "Of course," I said.

That Saturday around 11:00 a.m., I jumped into my Toyota Tacoma and drove the hour to Estes Park, in the mountains near Rocky Mountain National Park. She met me at the main building. We had Mexican food for lunch, saw a dollar movie in the afternoon, and hung out, getting to know each other until it was time to bring her back for her curfew that night.

Each Tuesday and Thursday afternoon, I would make the drive to get her to have dinner with me. I'd also see her in the UMC on Wednesdays, and each Saturday was ours.

Quickly and easily, we fell in love with each other. Every opportunity we could be together, we would, and if the payphone was open at her school, she'd call me at night when we weren't together.

That whole time, I tried to be the best Christian I could be. I thought that was what she would want—to have a good, wholesome, Christian man. I tried my best.

After four months, we decided two very important things: I'd spend spring break with her at her parents' home in Florida, and that was where I'd ask her parents' permission to marry her.

The dates were set, the flights were booked, and we were ready.

She already had tickets from when she originally planned her school year, so I came in separately on a flight a day later into Fort Lauderdale airport. She was there, waiting for me. The next ten days were full of excitement, going to the beach every day, meeting her siblings, sitting on the car hood as planes landed, going to church, and—between repeatedly driving over a landscape light in the driveway and consequently replacing it—asking her dad for his daughter's hand in marriage.

I liked her dad, Stephan (pronounced Stef-ahn; he was Swiss), a lot, and he liked me. He saw in me the same real and honorable devotion for his daughter that he felt when he had asked a young Gigi's father the same permission. That day, after making me sweat for a bit and talking to his wife, his answer came.

"Yes, of course, you can marry Jerushah," he said.

I was relieved and started to let out a long breath, but then he continued.

"But not yet."

Mr. Tchividjian knew if we got married while she was in Colorado, she might never return to her home in Florida. He suggested the fall would be better because she'd be finished with her one-year school and be back home. We both agreed, and I ran to tell Jerushah as he went to tell her mother.

That night at dinner, they toasted to us, and I was welcomed as part of the family.

Back in Colorado, we went back to our routine of Tuesdays, Wednesdays, Thursdays, and Saturdays and missed each other terribly on the days in between. We saw all sorts of movies together: *Jerry McGuire* at the $1 theater, *Dante's Peak, Fools Rush In, Liar Liar,*

and *Good Will Hunting*. We had cheap meals at Taco Bell and moderately expensive ones at Pasta Jays. As the weather warmed, we walked the Boulder Creek Trail and had coffee on The Hill. Before we knew it, her school year was over and she and Olivia went to pack up for the long drive home. I met up with them to see them off.

"Be safe," I said.

"We will be."

"I'll finish the semester and then head down," I said.

"That's the plan," said Jerushah.

"I'm going to miss you."

"Kyle, I'm going to miss you, too," she said. "But we'll see each other in a few weeks."

"Yeah," I said sullenly. "I know we will. It'll just be a while."

"She put her hand on mine and looked me in the eyes. "I love you. I'll see you soon."

While I finished up my classes over the next few weeks, we rarely talked. I tried to call her, but it was too early—she was still driving home. We spoke when she arrived but didn't yet make plans. Then it started getting hard to reach her. She had gone into full Florida beach summer mode and was having fun. Her parents didn't have call waiting, and on the off chance when I would get through, I would have to leave a message with her thirteen-year-old brother, who never gave her the message. During the days, she'd be at Deerfield Beach with Olivia, tanning in the Florida sun. The time change was hard, and we just couldn't sync up. In an age before texting, mobile phones, and email, we fizzled.

I never ended up getting to Florida that summer.

11 | ZEPHANIAH

"The LORD your God is with you, he is mighty to save."
—Zephaniah 3:17

I was distraught. I had lost touch with the love of my life. I had called and got nothing in return. I was unsure if she was merely busy, not getting my messages, or avoiding me on purpose. It took me too long to realize that I was holding out hope for something that would never come. Jerushah and I were finished.

I immediately went into a depression. Holed up in my bedroom, I spent the days on the floor, crying. That woman had validated that I was not only lovable, but I also had something to give to her. I had fallen madly in love, asked her dad if I could marry her, and even started wedding planning for that fall. I had begun the process of transferring schools to be near her, applying all over the Southeast to schools like the University of South Carolina, University of Florida, Florida Atlantic, and more. Now my reason to transfer was all gone, and I was gutted. Depression seeped in quickly and furiously. If I wasn't crying, I was sleeping, and I definitely wasn't eating.

The thought had crossed my mind to fly to Florida to try to

see what happened, but to buy tickets from Colorado was unusually high—over a grand—and even if I could afford it, I had no clue where her parents lived—I never knew the address. All I knew was that she was in Coral Springs, near Deerfield Beach. I thought I could hang out at the beach until I saw her but scratched that idea. So, staying in bed seemed like the best thought I could come up with.

I had lost about fifteen pounds in nearly three weeks from not eating. All I would do was curl up on the floor or on my bed, watch a few old VHS movies, and think about her. I was getting weaker by the day, as all I would have was coffee and whatever scraps my roommates left. Nothing was shaking me from that depression—if I ever gave anything an opportunity to.

Then my roommate shoved some letters under my bedroom door. I recognized a hand-written envelope and opened it up.

> Dear Kyle,
> The Lord put you on my heart this morning,
> and I think you should read this verse: Zephaniah 3:17
> In Him,
> Heather

I had met Heather when her father had spoken at family camp during the summer of my climbing accident in the mountains, but I hadn't spoken to her for nearly a year or so.

I ran to my bookshelf, yanked down my Bible, and found the verse smack dab in the middle of the book. I hadn't even heard of Zephaniah, but I started reading that verse, and then I read the chapter voraciously. Then I read it again and again and again. I broke down and cried.

"The LORD your God is with you, the Mighty Warrior who saves. He will take great delight in you; in his love, he will no longer rebuke you but will rejoice over you with singing."

I had wanted to die that morning before I read that verse. I had felt rejected and worthless. On top of it all, my shame was wrapped up in being a fake. Was that why we had drifted apart? Was I pretending to be the Christian I thought she wanted? Or did she merely not love me anymore? It was on replay in my head, and I couldn't turn it off. But that verse showed me that I was not alone.

We are not alone. Jesus loves us. He rejoices over us in song; he quiets us with his love! No matter how dirty we are—or think we are—the Lord of lords wants to cuddle us up and sing to us. How beautiful is that? That's the picture I imagine. Jesus gathers me in his arms like a dad to his young son, and sings over me, and loves me. My restlessness and anxiety were quieted by his love. Nothing removes us from his love. Nothing ever will. That's the promise he makes to us.

Maybe that was the lesson I needed to learn. I was not following him with my heart but with legality. I was telling my girlfriend that I had a quiet time with God every day, although I didn't, that I was praying for us as a couple, when in reality, I was just holding on for dear life. I wasn't trusting Jesus at all—I was doing it on my own, and still, when I failed and flailed, he undoubtedly collected me in his big arms, squeezed me tight, and loved me.

I wished I could say life has been peaches and cream ever since, but truthfully that was the first of many, many, *many* times he would show himself to me when I was humbled and broken. That was merely the first. That summer, I tattooed that very verse on my left calf in Hebrew to serve as a constant reminder to me that he takes great delight in me:

יְהֹוָה אֱלֹהַיִךְ בְּקִרְבֵּךְ גִּבּוֹר יוֹשִׁיעַ יָשִׂישׂ עָלַיִךְ בְּשִׂמְחָה יַחֲרִישׁ בְּאַהֲבָתוֹ יָגִיל עָלַיִךְ בְּרִנָּה׃

Over time, that tattoo has become just another mark on my body amidst many tattoos on my arms and legs. However, every once in a while, I felt a tug in my spirit toward him, and I would look down, hear the verse in my head, and remember how I have been redeemed.

There was a great baseball player on the Minnesota Twins team named Chuck Knoblach. He played second base and earned Rookie of the Year in 1991, the same year the Twins won the World Series. He later earned a Golden Glove for fielding at second base. He was spectacular to watch, and the Yankees thought so, too. He caught their eye, and they offered him a large you-can't-turn-it-down amount of money to come play for them. He went, but the pressure of playing major league ball in the biggest market with unrelenting fans ended up getting to him, and he started to lose focus.

He tried so hard to be a Yankee and live up to the fans' expectations that the more he tried, the worse he got. He started to lose his ability to throw the ball to first base. He could field quickly from his reflexes, but when he picked up the ball to make the throw, he was too much in his head and would miss the first baseman by a mile. After a while, they moved him to the outfield, but then he couldn't hit his cutoff man when throwing the ball back into the infield. During one game, he committed three errors in a single inning, so he walked off the field, through the tunnel, into the parking lot, and left the stadium fully clothed in his uniform and cleats. He eventually was traded from team to team and ultimately retired from baseball with little fanfare.

Knoblach was a great player who lost his focus. He tried to be something he thought was bigger than life: a Yankee. All they wanted him to do was hit, field, and throw—that was who he was and how he was most gifted. However, he lost focus and tried to be someone different, someone bigger. When he did, he literally couldn't do anything else but worry—and fail.

When we lose sight of Jesus, when we sin or lose our way, we end up losing our focus. We wonder what others think of us from the stands, and we try to fix the fact that we can't throw to first, not the mental issue, which is the real problem. We put all this effort behind something that will never yield success. The harder we try to impress, the further we miss the mark and overthrow the first baseman. Even when we break from our own indulgence, greed, or selfishness, we are still left vulnerable, ashamed, tired, and sad. Then we hide. We lie. We avoid it altogether. When Adam and Eve ate of the Tree of the Forbidden Fruit, they hid in shame. I did the same.

I was so wrapped up in dating Billy Graham's granddaughter that I lost focus on Jesus. I tried and tried, but I kept missing the mark, and in the end, it cost me the one person who truly loved me for me. I didn't know if we merely lost touch in the fun of a youthful summer or if it was purposeful, but through it all, I was still missing my cutoff man from my wild throws to first base.

Zephaniah's prophetic words snapped me out of a depression, and the tattoo served as a reminder, but it would be a long time before I ever learned how to fully appropriate myself to the Lord and trust him wholly.

12 | JOHNNY CASH

*"I wear the black for those who've never read or listened
to the words that Jesus said."*
—Johnny Cash, "The Man in Black"

A Young Life friend, and former badminton player, Paul, loved country music and the old rockabilly that his dad played while growing up in the plains of Sterling, Colorado. They'd listen to Merle Haggard, Carl Perkins, and Jerry Lee Lewis. His favorite—by far— was Johnny Cash, and he had heard that the Boulder Theater was going to host him and his wife, June, so Paul said to me, "This is your chance to find a way to get back in touch with Jerushah."

Paul knew that Jerushah had told me stories about how Johnny would play in their living room growing up, just for fun. He was good friends with Dr. Graham, Jerushah's grandfather, and often spent holidays with her mom and dad in Florida.

One time when her grandfather walked in sporting a new leather coat, she said, "Daddy Bill, that's a good-looking jacket." His reply was humble and modest, much like the man himself. "Thanks," he said. "My friend, John, gave it to me."

He meant Johnny Cash.

Paul had remembered these stories and thought that was our chance. We had to go.

We bought the tickets for fourteen dollars apiece at a Ticketmaster window at the Macy's customer service counter in the Crossroads Mall later that day. The concert would be around the corner. We couldn't wait. Paul wanted to see Cash himself, but I wanted to get Jerushah's mom's phone number, so I could get to Jerushah. Paul told me later he was kidding—there would be no way to meet Cash. But he had sparked an idea.

The week leading up to the show, I thought of ways I could get to the Man in Black. I called his record company, the venue, and even his latest recording studio. Finally, someone took pity on me and gave me Lou Robin's phone number, his longtime manager.

"Hello?" said a voice on the other end of the line.

"Uh, hello. Is this Mr. Robins?" I said.

"This is Lou Robins. Who am I speaking with?"

"Well, sir, this is going to sound crazy," I started and began my story: There was this girl, and we fell in love. We were engaged, and she moved home. Somehow we lost touch, and I didn't know how to get ahold of her.

"Okay, son," he said. "How can *I* help you?"

I had forgotten to tell him about the link to Mr. Cash.

"Oh! Right. Well, sir, she's Billy Graham's granddaughter, and I believe Mr. Cash knows Dr. Graham well. I just thought that—" he cut me off before I finished my sentence.

"Dr. Graham? Why didn't you say so, son?" he said. "Hey, now where are you located?"

"I'm in Boulder, Colorado, sir."

"Boulder? Well, this just gets better. John is coming to Boulder next week!"

I let him think it was his idea. I wasn't going to jeopardize this opportunity.

"Can I get you tickets to the show?" he asked.

"Well, sir, I actually have tickets. That's why I called you. I am wondering if I could have a word with Mr. Cash while I'm there."

"Son, whatever you need."

It was getting surreal, "Okay, what do I do?"

"John will play a few songs, then June will come up. As soon as he leaves the stage, come down to the backstage door, and I'll find you," he said.

"That's it?" I said. "I can do that."

I spelled my name for him, gave him my home phone number, and asked if I needed to check in with him before the show. He assured me that I didn't need to.

On the night of the show, I was so nervous. I told Paul to bring something for him to sign just in case we saw him—but I didn't mention the rendezvous I had set up with his manager. He still didn't think it was possible to meet Johnny Cash and almost left his expensive box set at home, but I told him the chances were high. He rolled his eyes and grabbed the Man in Black CD box set.

Just as sure as Lou had said, John came out and sang first, starting with "Folsom Prison Blues," "Riders in the Sky," "Sunday Mornin' Comin' Down," and "Get Rhythm," the last one with June. Knowing he'd need extra oxygen at this altitude, he stepped off stage, allowing June to sing a few of her songs, solo, while he went to his bus.

I jumped up from my seat. *This is it!* I thought. I ran down to the main floor, found the long hallway to the right of the stage, and followed it to the back. I told the security guard that Lou told me to find him, who appeared seconds later.

"Hi! I'm Kyle."

"Hello!" said the older man. "Are you ready?"

"Can I get my friend to come with me? He's a big fan," I asked.

"Well, okay. But you need to hurry."

"Okay, I'll be right back!" I said, my words trailing off as I ran back up the ramp, through the crowd, up the stairs, and to my row to find Paul. I knelt down next to him in the aisle.

"Paul, come with me."

"Duford," he said, "I'm watching this."

"Paul, listen to me." I looked at him sternly, chest breathing quickly from my run. "If you don't come with me right now, you're going to miss your chance to meet Johnny Cash."

He shot me a look, wondering if I was completely full of crap or not. He must've decided it was worth the risk. He got up and started to come with me.

"Oh," I said, "your CD set!"

He snagged his boxed set and followed me back down to Lou, who was patiently waiting at the same door in which I left him.

"Okay, sir," I said, "We're ready."

Lou led Paul and me through the backstage maze of the Boulder Theater, then out the back door that emptied into the alley where his tour bus sat. The distance from the back of the building to the bus door couldn't have been more than twelve feet, but in that space between were dumpsters, trash, and an awful smell that stayed with me long afterward.

Lou knocked a secret knock on the door: *rap-rappity-rap-rap-rap*. A second later, it opened, and there stood the Man in Black himself, on the second step from the top, looking down at us. He looked massive. He was holding an oxygen mask over his face, which he briefly removed to say, "Hello, fellas. Thanks, Lou, I'll take them from here."

Mr. Cash led us back into the bus, where we stood next to an oxygen tank as he periodically sucked on that mask between speaking.

"So, which one of you boys is engaged to that sweet Jerushah?"

Well, I used to be.

"Oh, I am, sir. I'm Kyle." He shook my hand with a hard, firm, tight grip that could instruct any boy how to be a man. "This is my friend, Paul. He's a big fan."

"Hello, Paul, I'm John," said The Man. "Nice to meet you."

Paul couldn't move. That was his hero, standing before him, shaking his hand. He was in awe.

"So, how's the family?" said John, meaning Jerushah's.

"Oh, everyone's really good. They send their love," I lied.

"Gigi and Stephan are really great people and good friends," he continued, meaning her parents.

"Yeah, they're the best," I said.

Paul's mouth was still agape, staring at him.

"What brings you here?" he asked.

"Oh, I go to school here, at CU—you know, the University of Colorado? She just moved back home at the beginning of summer."

"Didn't she go to school out here, too? Up in the mountains?"

Damn, he was closer to them than I thought, he knew more details, and I was definitely burying myself in the allusion that I was still with her.

"Yup, Ravencrest."

"Good thing, there. To read the Bible for school. I bet she learned a lot."

"Yes, sir, I believe she did."

I was losing my nerve. I inadvertently turned this conversation into a catch-up with Johnny Cash—of all people—about the Tchividjian family. How was I going to steer this back to the questions I needed to ask, which was "Do you know how to convince Jerushah to be with me again?"

Just then, that secret knock on the door came, but that time, instead of waiting for the door to open, Lou walked in without John coming for him.

"Okay, boys, it's time for Mr. Cash to go back on stage," he said to us. "John, are you ready?" said Lou.

"Yeah, all right. Well, guys," he said, "Kyle, Paul, it sure was a pleasure meeting the man who is going to marry sweet Jerushah and his friend. Please tell her and her parents that June and I send our best. We'll be sure to be praying for you two."

"Yes, yes, yes, sir," I said. "Thank you." I had lied to the Man in Black.

We were ushered to the door when I realized Paul hadn't said a word and we needed to get something out of this experience.

"Mr. Cash?" I asked. "Would you be able to sign Paul's CD? He's a big fan.

"Sure," he said.

I had to pry the box out of Paul's hand and give it to Johnny, who merely signed his signature, "Johnny Cash," in black pen on a black box. You could only ever see it if you held it just right in the light.

We all walked out together, through the garbage stench, and back into the theater. When we got to the stage, John shook our hands again, turned right as June on stage saw him and announced him back to the crowd. Paul and I went straight, thanked Lou profusely, and went back to our seats.

Paul and I were speechless but for different reasons. He tightly clutched that box set in his hands until he got home and didn't say much along the way. He was stunned at what had just happened. I was stunned, too. I had blown my opportunity.

A few songs later, Johnny sang "Ring of Fire" about his heart's burning love for June. *It sure would be nice to feel that again,* I thought. *It sure would be nice.*

13 | COFFEE ON THE HILL

"'Cause no one knows you like they know you [...]
The truth is there's nothing like old friends
'Cause you can't make old friends"
—Ben Rector, "Old Friends"

It was not long after the Cash/Carter concert in 1997 when I was hanging out at my favorite coffee shop in Boulder, Buchanan's Coffee Pub on The Hill. The Hill was the neighborhood sandwiched between the foothills of the Rockies to the west and the university campus to the east. It was full of college stores, burrito joints, Albums on the Hill, where we once saw Dave Matthews, and the Fox Theatre, where we saw Dave play. The Hill was where students would head for lunch, drinks, or art supplies. It was surrounded by sorority and fraternity houses. Not far from the south end of The Hill was where JonBenét Ramsey had spent her last night.

Buchanan's sat on Pennsylvania Avenue, diagonally across from The Sink, where Robert Redford once worked in the 50s.

J.W. "Buck" Buchanan probably knew Redford, given their similar age, but rather he went into real estate and eventually opened the coffee shop in the early 90s. I had once designed his new logo in exchange for one free coffee drink per day as long as I lived in town. My go-to: a 16 oz. iced vanilla latte, thank you.

I was sitting on the patio of Buck's coffee shop, swilling my latte and basking in the sun, when I saw a gorgeous Weimaraner tied up, waiting for his owner. He seemed friendly enough to pet, so I kneeled down on one knee and started to say "Hi," when—

"Hello," said the owner.

"Oh, hi," I said, standing up. "I'm sorry, I just think your dog is beautiful. I hope it's okay I said hi."

"Sure, sure."

"What's his name?"

"This is Roark."

"Roark?" I asked.

"From The Fountainhead. I'm a big Ayn Rand fan."

"He's gorgeous," I said.

"Thanks. I got him my freshman year. Probably a mistake, but he keeps me exercising—he needs the activity."

Something seemed oddly familiar about this person. *Did I go to class with him? Is he the boyfriend of a friend or something?*

"That sounds great. I heard they're great running dogs."

He nodded. "Yeah, I take them on the trail with me, you know, up Mount Sanitas? He loves that."

"Oh, brother, I can barely hike that," I said. "He runs that with you?"

"He loves it!" he said as he was untying Roark to go.

Then he said, "It was nice chatting with you," and he took Roark's leash in one hand, his coffee in the other, and started to walk away.

I couldn't shake the feeling. I knew this guy. "Hey," I called to him, "I'm sorry, but you look awfully familiar."

He turned around. "Yeah? I don't know from where."

"I'm Kyle," I said. "Maybe you just have a familiar face."

"Wait . . . Kyle . . . Duford?"

"Yeah, actually."

"I'm Josh."

"Where do I know you from, Josh? Class?"

"Kyle, Joshua—from Allentown."

"Whoa, Josh?" I hadn't seen him since middle school. We were told old wives' tales that he had run away from home. I hadn't seen him since . . . 1989? "Man, what are you doing in Boulder?" I asked.

"I go to school here—well, I *went* to school here. I just graduated."

"What was it, sixth grade since we saw each other?"

"Something like that," he said. "Remember your twelfth birthday party when we went camping? Where was that—"

"Otter Lake! That was so much fun. You hurled a cherry bomb into the woods and set the leaves on fire."

"I had forgotten about that," he said. "Well, let's keep that between us—I'm headed to law school."

"Staying here, I imagine?" I asked.

"No, I'm heading to Michigan. I got into law school there."

"That sounds great," I said. "Well, it'd be good to catch up this summer before you head out."

"Actually, I just took a break from packing to come up here. I leave this weekend."

"You're kidding me. We at least need to have a beer."

"I wish I could," said Josh. "I'm behind as it is. I have to leave my apartment by Monday. Then I'm heading out."

He sat back down and tied Roark back up. We talked about the good times we'd had in school, at the JCC day camp, and riding our bikes or skateboards around West Allentown. It had seemed so long ago but also so recent.

He was older now, but the spirit and spunk he had as a kid were still there. I couldn't shake the feeling, but it felt like God was saying through Josh, "Leave him alone. He's my friend," as if God was still somehow protecting me. I had fallen so far in such a short time, I didn't have direction. God knew it.

Through our time together over an hour or so, I got the same feeling I had when we were kids: unabashed friendship. As if Josh were wrapped in Jesus and whispering, "I'm still here. I'll find you."

14 | STRONG THE TIES
"That's the beauty of college these days.
You can major in Game Boy if you know how to bullshit."
—James 'Droz' Andrews, *PCU*

With a good summer behind me, I was able to start to focus on moving forward. That was all well and good, but I needed a place to stay. I had to vacate the rental home I was currently staying in by the end of August, and the next semester was about to begin, so I was in a hurry.

I took a break from looking for apartments to go to an FCA event with a few friends. The Fellowship of Christian Athletes is a ministry primarily on college and university campuses that provides a place for student athletes who believe in Jesus a place to worship, be together, and bring friends to hear the gospel in a safe environment. I went because I was tired of being home, searching the classifieds for apartments, or feeling like I was in the way while the owner was readying the house for sale.

It was there, after that meeting, that some Young Life

friends asked me about the search. "Bad," I said. "And I have only a few weeks left before I get booted."

"See that guy over there?" they pointed. "He's the president of AGO, the Christian Fraternity, and they have an open room."

I met the decathlete they pointed out and his friend, and we struck up a conversation.

"Hi, I was told you're looking for a roommate?"

"Hey! Yeah, we are. We have a few people looking at it, though. I'm Chris."

"Hi, Chris, I'm Kyle."

"I'm Gumby," said the lanky guy next to him.

"Gumby?" I said.

"Well, yeah. I mean, it's Tyler. But you can call me Gumby."

I shook his hand. "When can I see it?" I asked

"Anytime," said Chris. "We're heading there now."

He wrote down the address, and I showed up shortly afterward. The room was actually an old wine cellar that was carpeted and enclosed and included in the unit by adding an outdoor hallway from the backdoor to the cellar. It was separated but in the house just the same. Rent was $250 a month. I took it on the spot.

Part of the deal was that I'd be out of the house on Sunday nights and Wednesday nights while fraternity gatherings were held in the main room. I wasn't allowed in my dungeon, either, for fear I'd hear secret information in the room above my cave. I agreed.

Chris was better known as "Wally," and we took an immediate liking to each other. He was close to my age, a runner and athlete, and as down to earth as you can imagine. He was tall, over six feet, thin as a rail with a blond, receding hairline. He was also a rabid Buffaloes fan. Nearly every shirt, sweatshirt, or hat he owned was emblazoned with the CU logo.

"Why are you called Wally?" I asked him while he showed me around the rest of the house.

"From *Leave it to Beaver*," he said. "You know the old show?"

Of course, I did. My brother made me watch it in between reruns of *Hogan's Heroes* and *Get Smart*.

"Apparently, it's because I'm so wholesome." He shrugged.

"Okay, so what about Gumby?" I asked.

"You met him. Doesn't he look like Gumby?"

We chuckled, and then he continued the tour, introducing me to all the brothers who lived in the Alpha Gamma Omega house. There was Duke and Wittenburg off the main room, Vatto and Slurpee near the stairs, Wally roomed with Tyson, and Falcon with Gumby upstairs in the "attic." There were other brothers who lived in the dorms or in another home together. Guys were named after their love of activities (soccer, Spanish, philosophy), their service (Falcon was in the US Marines), or characteristics (Duke was as slow-talking and moving as the cartoon dog, Marmaduke). All in all, there were fifteen active members, all from the first year the fraternity had started on campus, the year prior. Each semester they were lucky to add one or two more members. After curiosity and exhaustion from leaving my home twice a week got the better of me, I became one of them.

I had no idea those would be the men who would pour into me over the next two years.

My pledge class included Elway, the football lover, and Watson, the smart detective-like personality. Ruck was our pledge master, and on numerous occasions, I resisted his "orders" as I was four years his senior and I couldn't see the point of doing push-ups because I couldn't remember the fraternity started in 1927 or that it was UCLA and not Cal Berkeley. Wally became my big brother, and since he was the president that semester, I got away with murder. I mean, they could kick me out but not evict me.

Pledging took the entire semester before we entered initiation and would become active brothers. I joked that the hazing portion would probably consist of memorizing scripture for hours at a time then reciting Leviticus by memory. But initiation was actually a fun, bonding experience, and I eventually got through the semester and became a full-time member.

The days leading up to the first day of the following spring semester were fun. Students were returning from holiday vacation, and the town was starting to buzz again from its sleepy state when no students were there. As students returned, many organizations would go through the campus and "chalk" the paths with messages: "Join Student Democrats," "Ultimate Frisbee Try-outs Next Week on the Quad," or "Join the Christ-Centered Fraternity," which was ours with a local phone number—our house line—just below it.

I thought that was a mistake, chalking the entire campus under cover of dark for students to impersonally see in the morning. Even from a non-Christian childhood, I knew this wasn't the right thing to do because, from experience, I knew that unless you had grounds in which to speak the gospel, it wouldn't land. *Rather*, I thought, *we should do Jim Rayburn's idea, the founder of Young Life, and "earn the right to be heard," or make relationships before proclaiming the gospel— much like Mike had done with me years earlier.* They disagreed.

And although I protested, Wally was having none of it. "We're chalking! We do this each semester."

"Yeah," I said, "but that's not how you met me, Watson, or Elway this year!"

"But it's what we do," said Vatto, the current pledge master.

I watched them do it with my hands in my pockets on a cold night. They chalked *everywhere*. It would've been hard not to see the messages, even from outer space.

We got home, exhausted, ate some Jalinos pizza, and sat in the main room when the phone rang. Tyson grabbed it but handed it to Wally to answer.

"AGO," he said.

On the other line, I could hear the guy talk in a *Jerky Boys* voice, making a go at us. "Yeah, I want to be in your sorority or whatever. I want to know Jesus!"

It was clearly a mock call, but Wally held his ground. "Well, we have an informational meeting on Tuesday night—" He was cut off.

"No, I want to be in the Jesus sorority now!" the voice said.

Now I could hear the laughter. "Wally! Hang up!" I yelled, but he kept up his gentle demeanor.

Tyson snatched the phone and hung up.

Minutes later, the phone rang again. I jumped up and said, "I'll get it."

"Yeah, I want to be in your sorority with Jesus!"

My blood boiled. "Listen, you sonofabitch, I know you're sitting in your nice apartment that your daddy paid for while you're getting bad grades and can't get a date with a girl, so you listen carefully. I'm not as devout as these guys here, so why don't I meet you right now and show you a little Jesus, you motherf—"

Wally slapped the back of my head and knocked the phone, sending it flying across the room, hitting the wall, and making the battery pop out and end the call.

The fight that ensued between us was legendary and remains in fraternity lore twenty-five years later. We pushed each other onto tables and flipped dishes at each other, basically destroying the living room and kitchen. Wally tackled me into the wall, tried to punch me. I landed one square on his jaw. Tyson watched with both excitement and, from my vantage point, a little envy—he had kind of always wanted to punch Wally. Had there been cellphones with cameras back then, it would've been on Instagram within minutes. At some point, we ended up on the floor, in the kitchen, leaning against the upended table. We sat together, exhausted, and laughed. We realized then that we were all different types.

Two weeks later, our new president, Cy, or "Falcon," was called into the marine's active reserves and abandoned his post. An emergency election was held, and I was put up alongside Wally as the two potential presidential nominees, nominated by our brothers.

There was no precedent for this. Though no active member had gone immediately from pledge to president in seventy-two years, technically, I was filling a vacancy well into the school year. The nationals agreed. The vote was held, and I beat Wally in a landslide, with every active vote coming my way, except one—his.

Our friendship was a bit awkward after that night, but we mended it over the course of that semester as I tried to lead boys into becoming men. It was hard since I was not yet the man I wanted to be.

There's something that happens when you're sought out to be included in a group. There becomes an inherent sense of belonging and possibly brotherhood when you're accepted.

I can think of Andrew and Peter, the fisherman in the Bible. What right did they have to be with Jesus? To be included in his tribe? Yet when Jesus found the brothers sitting on the side of the lake, cleaning their nets, he accepted them immediately for who they were. I can't imagine that after a long day of hard, hot, back-breaking work—with how many fish or how few we don't know—they must've been a sight. Fishermen, cleaning and gutting fish and their nets by hand? Surely this was smelly work. Have you been next to a fishmonger in Seattle's Pike Place market? Or in an open-air seafood market? It's quite the smell. The pungent, fishy smell of freshly caught—or cleaned—fish is something else. Now imagine doing that all day long, every day of the week but the Sabbath, and not having the modern hygienic soaps or shampoos we have today? I can smell the fish now.

That didn't faze Jesus. He wasn't worried about who he brought into his inner circle. Fishermen, merchants, even the loathed tax collectors. He sat men around his table who were hardened by either life, work, or the people around them.

Like the apostles, the men of AGO welcomed me—and others—in a way astonishing to both Christian groups and to the other fraternities on campus. A philosopher, a scientist, an athlete, a marine, a theologian, a rebel, a jazz saxophone player, the list could go on.

From the outside world, Jesus looked crazy, not so much as to what he was proclaiming—which was mind-shifting in its own right—but because of who he took in. These men broke bread together, drank together, lived together. They were the original AGO men.

One of my best friends to this day is another AGO alumni, Chum—I've never been sure of what his full name is, but it's something of Filipino-American origin. He was at the UCLA chapter, and we met one fall when I traveled to Los Angeles for a nationwide fraternity football tournament. With a penchant for good design and art direction, we've followed similar career paths.

Back in his own UCLA school days, he made shirts for all his brothers—which outnumbered our Boulder active members by double. The front of the shirt was printed simply with "AGO," and on the back of the t-shirt, "Come join a fraternity who immortalized a guy who drank, partied with the hearty, and hung out with prostitutes." Whoa, did that ever get a response! Such a response, in fact, that I stole it for a local *Colorado Daily* advertisement.

That was Jesus. He invited them all—drunks, taxpayers, and prostitutes. He fed them all at his table.

I ended up serving two more full semesters as the president, and although my faith was continuing to crumble and I was walking away from the Lord, I'll never forget those men in my life. In fact, my big brother, Wally, little brother "Hats," and *his* little brother, Bobby, and I are all still friends with each other. Four generations of "brothers."

God took a broken, depressed boy in a man's body and dropped him off at his one-and-only FCA meeting, where he met his future landlord, brother, and friend. I've been a close-minded person most of my life but opening myself up to these fifteen or so frat guys was a way he continued to speak into my life.

I wonder, if we all looked around and took chances with one another, what might happen in our lives?

15 | RAISING THE BAR

"Fight for things you care about but do it in a
way that will lead others to join you."
— Ruth Bader Ginsburg

It was in the wake of 9/11 that I started a triathlon magazine while I was living in Minneapolis. I had just lost a bunch of weight to train for—and compete in—my first of many triathlons. I wanted to help others use this sport to be their best selves and thought a magazine was the best way to go. While the original plan was to launch it five years later, the decision after 9/11 was to just do it then. *Why not, I thought? What do I have to lose? Let's try it in five months!*

Somehow, miraculously, others agreed. Some of the most notable writers, *Sports Illustrated* photographers, USA Triathlon national coaches, and even six-time Ironman World Champion, Dave Scott, wrote in that first issue. Everyone wanted to be a part of it.

We launched as a national publication in late April 2002. In a sleuth-like, Trojan horse fashion, instead of trying to go toe to toe with the other two big magazines, the strategy was simple: go thin but wide. We carefully found the address of every triathlon, cycling, swim, or running store in the United States—an exhausting effort to find literally everyone when most had yet to discover the internet—and sent every one of them exactly three issues, each adhered with a sticker saying, "STORE COPY: Not for resale." Along with that, instead of sponsoring a large race such as the Escape from Alcatraz or Mrs. T's Pierogies Chicago Triathlon, each with thousands of racers who would've received a free issue, we chose to sponsor the smaller, backyard triathlons in small American towns all over the country. These ma and pa triathlons at YMCAs or neighborhood parks may not have been well-known, but the people who raced them were the ones we wanted to reach: parents, newbies, collegiates—the everyman. We sponsored hundreds of these triathlons, each with two hundred or fewer entrants. We didn't have to pay a dime, and they welcomed this value-add to the race packets. Sure, *Triathlete* magazine could sponsor the six thousand racers at Alcatraz, but our little magazine eclipsed that number of giveaways in a single state like Illinois by sponsoring forty or so smaller events individually. We did this in every state in the nation, thus dwarfing the bigger magazine's reach by a landslide. We just did it like we were eating an elephant: one bite at a time.

In the wake of that strategy, two things happened. We immediately became an overnight contender, and we inadvertently became the people's magazine for triathlon. In that same wake, some bigger, well-known companies wanted to place advertisements for the next issue, scheduled for June: Asics, Reebok, Cervélo, and many more. But not all of them.

I always wanted to take on ads from companies in which I believed in and used. I'd rather have Adidas, Timex, Oakley, and Trek because those were the brands I followed into the sport and hoped they'd see the vision for what we wanted to accomplish. And for nutrition? I wanted CLIF Bar.

CLIF Bar was on the top of its game at the time. It was in

the middle of a battle with PowerBar over control of the endurance sports market—more like an all-out war—and the two companies vied for market share, mere miles apart from each other. PowerBar's office tower loomed large in Berkeley, California, and on a clear day, you could see the CLIF Bar office in nearby Emeryville.

PowerBar had already come to the table to place ads through an intermediary broker who booked a few inside-the-book, right-hand-side advertisements. I was grateful, but with the burgeoning CLIF Bar right behind them in the market, I wanted both.

I started to call the CLIF Bar office as often as I could. I tried sports marketing, product marketing, global marketing—whoever would take a call. Sometimes I was forced to leave a message. Many times they'd never answer. A few times they hung up on me.

"Never heard of you." *Click.*

"Our budget is spent for the year." *Click.*

"Our agency places all of our buys; try them." *Click.*

I was relentless, however. There was something about the allure of CLIF that clipped a nerve in me. I dialed the agency. It went something like this:

I'd call the agency. They'd forward me to the account manager. The account manager would send me back to CLIF. CLIF would tell me to tell the account manager that they had okayed it. I'd call the agency back and get forwarded to the account manager. The account manager told me to fax something to them. I'd fax the required documents. I'd call back. Get forwarded and told to verify receipt with CLIF HQ. CLIF instructs me to deal with the agency. I called the agency, and around we went.

At that point, it had been at least two weeks of this back and forth. So much so that when the secretary saw a Minnesota number, I imagined they'd either cautiously pick it up or ignore it. It was that bad.

Finally, I got through to the account manager again. After some more instructions on some ridiculous list of tasks, she said,

"Good luck!" and started to hang up, while in the background, before the phone hit the receiver, I heard her say "I told him to call CLIF back—" and I heard them laughing.

I was the brunt of the joke.

I sat for a second in the ridicule and shame of this realization that I would never get CLIF Bar to advertise, and my anger started to well up inside me. I picked up the phone and dialed their main office.

"Hello, Clif Bar," said the voice.

"Hi. You don't know me. But I've been trying to get a hold of anyone there who can talk to me about advertising," I said.

"Hold and I'll transfer you to marketing."

"*Wait!*" I yelled. "No, thanks, that doesn't help. I've been to the marketing department."

She was confused. "Then where do you want to be transferred?"

"I don't care," I said. "All I know is that I just launched a magazine that no one there seems to think is going places. I'll probably be a nobody, and the magazine may not ever go anywhere, but on the off chance it does, I want you to find someone in the office who gives a shit about possibly angering a magazine editor which may—one day—forever ban CLIF Bar from all its pages!"

My heart was thumping through my chest. I knew I had just alienated that company forever. I waited for the dial tone to come when I heard her say, "Let me see what I can do."

A minute went by. Then five. It seemed like an eternity. I was starting to think it was another joke.

Then a voice came to the line. "Hello, this is Tim."

"Hi, Tim, I'm Kyle from *americanTRI* magazine."

"Hi, Kyle," said the pleasant voice. "What's up?"

"Well," I said. "What were you told?"

"Just to get on the phone. Someone was really upset. Was that you?"

"Yeah, I suppose, Tim. I was originally talking to the

marketing department—"

"Oh," he said on the other end.

"Oh?" I questioned.

"I'm in finance, but . . ." he paused, "tell me what's going on."

I told Tim the story in as much detail as possible. I told him that the tri club I led used CLIF Bars to train, I'd always been a fan, and I was getting the runaround from his colleagues and from some ad agency they used. Then I told him about the laughing. That got his attention.

"Wait . . . what? They laughed?"

"I'm pretty sure," I said. "And It was definitely at my expense."

Tim didn't take much time to say anything after that, just that he'd get back to me. For some reason, I believed it that time.

The very next day, I was called to the main office of our office complex because I had received a fax for the magazine. I nearly fell over when I saw it. The fax was an insertion order for four ads over the next four issues, all back covers at full-rate card, which was our published rate of $6,500 for that placement.

Tim came through in a big way.

When I got back to our office the phone was ringing. It was Tim. He had just sent a fax and wanted to make sure we had received it.

"I can't believe you did this," I said.

"No one should have been treated that way," he said. "Especially someone who enjoys CLIF Bar like you do. To be sure, you won't have to deal with the agency. My friend, Chris, works in the sports marketing department, and he'll be your contact from now on. I already spoke to him."

A few days later, about forty boxes of CLIF Bars showed up at the office. Not twelve-pack boxes you can buy in bulk, but boxes of twelve-packs. They were enough for a year or more. My daughter's third word inevitably was "bar" right after "mama" and "dada."

I was young and bold, sure, and while that had something

to do with it all, I wasn't living the life Jesus wanted for me. I had already shoved my faith in a hole and was following my desire to look good and become successful, not to glorify him. That would be a trait that would follow me for some time.

What Tim did was remarkable. He took a chance. He heard passion in my voice and rewarded it. He listened. He was kind. He calmed me down. He became my advocate. He found a solution.

I went on to sell my magazine to one of our competitors, *Inside Triathlon*, and I joined them as an editor. Tim would check up on me in my new role from time to time. When I met CLIF Bar Founder, Gary Erickson, at a Denver, Colorado, REI store, he didn't know me personally, but rather the story and my original magazine. And when I eventually moved to Oakland, California, a stone's throw from their Emeryville head office, Tim emailed me and asked if I needed anything. When I later applied to CLIF Bar, he ushered my resume to the right person even though I didn't end up being hired.

I have never met Tim. But he showed me some of the most amazing grace and kindness of anyone I have actually met. Why would someone who doesn't know me from Adam give a crap about me? Sure, a cynic would say that obviously, he wanted to advance the brand in the event that our little magazine became something. However, I couldn't imagine that in the days since we sold the magazine and left the magazine business entirely, that he had any desire to continue to help me.

The fact is, Tim didn't need to do anything. He most certainly didn't need to once I had left the endurance sports world and moved to California.

I have never seen Jesus—face to face, anyway—but I know he's there. I rely on him, and I need him to help me in my life. Many non-Christians ask me all the time how I can believe in something I have never seen. The short answer? I have seen the effects of what he has done in my life. I have seen his hand in my life. While I had already walked away from my faith when I encountered CLIF Bar, he was still working, and that time through Tim.

Because of his encouragement, I continued to press on. Having them on our back cover solidified that we were a player. It gave us validation and enough credibility to march on. Tim was in finance yet made magic happen.

I pray that I will do the same for other people who enter my life.

16 | CALLING IT EVEN

"I will give you a new heart and put a new spirit in you;
I will remove from you your heart of stone and give
you a heart of flesh."
—Ezekiel 36:26

I had first met Chris Carmichael, Lance Armstrong's former coach, at a fitness camp where I participated in a press junket outside Boone, North Carolina. It was 2005, and editors from all the endurance and adventure magazines were present to hear about Power-Bar's new hydration drink. We'd test our VO2 max, go run trails, learn about hydration, get more tests, run some more, then repeat. Carmichael was there to offer some celebrity cycling credibility.

A little background on Chris: as Armstrong's coach during the seven years in which he was atop the podium, Carmichael had rocketed from merely being known in the cycling community to an all-star super coach. One problem was now facing him, however, as Lance faded from view: Carmichael's coaching services were in less and less demand. The off-season was coming up, and it seemed a perfect time to tune up not only his body for next season but also his business, Carmichael Training Systems, a new strategy in an up-coming, post-Lance world.

Ever since Carmichael had coached the USA Men's Olympic Cycling Team, he had called Colorado Springs, Colorado, home. Its grand views of the Rockies and Pikes Peak, wide-open cycling spac-es, and high elevation make it a perfect place to house the Olympic Training Center, and conveniently, Carmichael's coaching business.

At this elevation of 6,000-feet, the body has less oxygen, causing you to fatigue more rapidly and get out of breath very quickly. At this altitude, however, the human body does something remarkable: it creates more red blood cells to help carry more oxy-gen. Consequently, when you return to a lower elevation where the oxygen is more available, the extra red blood cells you've built up help you last longer, go farther, and fatigue less. It's why so many teams train here and why so many endurance athletes dot Colorado's front range with home bases. The more you train high and race low, the better you'll do in competition.

But oxygen wasn't Chris's problem in the fall of 2005. It was staying relevant.

Enter his Editorial Director and word wizard, Grant Davis.

Davis had been an editor for *Men's Health, Stuff,* and *Outside* magazine, but when Carmichael tapped him to head up his editorial team, he took it. That was a big deal for him. Now my phone was ringing, and Davis was on the other end. I knew of Grant as much as he knew of me.

"Kyle?" said a soft-spoken voice.

"Yes, Grant? Nice to meet you," I said.

"I know we spoke about this briefly over email, but I'd love a chance to talk to you in person. Maybe we can do a ride together next week down here in the Springs?"

I had never had a job interview on a bicycle before, but nev-ertheless, why wouldn't I jump at a chance to be one more level closer to Lance? "Yeah, let me check my schedule . . . hold on a second, um . . ." I said as I ruffled some papers on my home office desk for effect, as if I were busy, "How about Tuesday?"

"Great, 10 a.m. sound okay? Bring your bike and kit. We have drink mix, water bottles, and showers," he said.

"Perfect, 10 a.m. it is. See you then."

The drive from Boulder to Colorado Springs isn't a hard one. It's basically one right turn off Highway 36, then a straight shot down the middle of the state, through Denver, until you get off your exit in the Springs. Depending on the traffic in Denver, however, it could take anywhere from one and a half to three hours, so I left extra early, bike loaded on the roof of my VW Jetta and partially wearing my Lycra getup with the rest of my gear in the passenger seat. I made sure I had everything with me: helmet, gloves, vest and jacket, gels, patch-kit, pump—everything. I was so bogged down with extra gear, it must've looked like I'd never ridden before. But the truth was I had never ridden with a group of former pros before, and I wanted to be ready, if not *look* ready.

Davis met me at the front door, greeted me, and showed me around. At six foot four inches, he towered over me. He wore glasses, had a receding dark head of hair, and was wearing a collared CTS shirt tucked into his pants. He moved methodically, not slowly, but with purpose. His long arms matched his frame, and I still remember the cadence of his arms moving fluidly as he walked me through the office, introducing me quickly to "Rutty" and Kevin, and pointing down the long hallway toward Chris's office, where the hall opened to two double doors to his domain, his desk squarely in the middle where he was seated, simultaneously reading something, and talking on the phone. *It must be Lance on the phone*, I figured.

There were rows of cubicles for coaches, another row for nutritionists, and a few admin people. The back of the building was enormous, with rows of shelving for the store, which included DVDs, shirts, accessories, and gear from their sponsors. A large area was reserved for the live spinning classes with about a dozen empty fluid trainers facing the same direction, waiting for bikes to adorn them, whereas the other side of the large room was for bike fitting, treadmill testing, or other forms of data gathering.

"You can change in here," pointed Davis, showing me the bathroom.

As he said that, I immediately became self-conscious; I felt awkward in my cycling "kit," my nearly skin-tight pink and white Lycra outfit. It was a T-Mobile jersey, the team of Jan Ulrich—Lance Armstrong's chief competitor in the Tour de France. *Yikes. What was I thinking?* All this preparation and I had chosen the one jersey not to wear. I might as well have walked into Nike headquarters wearing an Adidas tracksuit. If I could have completely changed my outfit, I would've, but instead, I finished getting ready, and we headed out.

Our ride together was epic, even without any pros riding. After riding from the office, we trolled through town, headed toward the mountains and through the Garden of the Gods. We ended up doing about a twenty-five-mile massive loop around town, finding a different way back into the Springs and finally arriving at the headquarters once again. Grant was riding on my left side when we passed a road to my right, the last turn back toward the office. He turned into me, forgetting to tell me when to turn. We bumped each other, flailed, and both managed to stay upright enough to have a laugh. That must've endeared me to him a little bit.

After getting back, I showered and got more presentable. We talked about my days at *Inside Triathlon*, our mutual love of cycling, and of course, the only two people we wanted to meet in real life: Lance and Bono from U2. I didn't have the heart to tell him mine were really Lance and Michael Stipe of R.E.M.

Then he shook my hand and said, "I'll send you some assignments and get you an email address this week; when can you get me five hundred words by?"

My shower had taken longer than our discussion about work. "I'm . . . hired?"

"Well, yeah, what did you think this was?"

"I thought it was an interview," I said.

"Oh, I did my due diligence ahead of time. I've read all your articles. I know you'd be perfect for us."

"Then what was the bike ride about?" I asked.

"Ha," he chuckled. "That was just a bike ride. Thought you might enjoy riding together."

"I can get you those five hundred words by Friday," I said. "Load me up!"

"Great, let's go down to Rutty's office and see what else he may need from you."

I spent the next year or so freelancing for Grant, Carmichael, and Rutty, who authors all of Chris's books, and though I never got a chance to meet Lance, I had made a meaningful friend in Grant.

When Carmichael contracted his editorial and nutritional teams due to budget cuts, I got Grant hired on where I worked at Examiner.com. After I was fired from Examiner, Grant got me a job writing and designing maps for the nation's state parks. The time I was head-hunted to be an editor for *Wild Blue Yonder* magazine, the in-flight magazine for Denver's Frontier Airlines, I recommended Grant—instead of me—and he was hired.

We then wrote a few articles together for *Outside* magazine and other publications and continued this back and forth lobbing of jobs to one another throughout the next fifteen years.

In the winter of 2007, I was in a rut. Balancing my life and figuring out what was next as a thirty-three-year-old with a failed marriage already under my belt and Christmas coming up without my daughter. Grant didn't care what I'd done or been through or the fact that now I was jobless and looking to show people I still had value. I wanted something epic to prove to myself that I still had some life left in me. So, Grant suggested a half-marathon, together, in the dark, in Colorado Springs. Quickly and foolishly, I agreed and made the drive down that Saturday afternoon to his house.

The starting point would be his home, which sat right near the trail. We'd run 13.1 miles through the trails with all our winter gear on, backpacks stuffed with solar blankets and food, and headlamps to light the way. We started off at around six o'clock in the evening, just before it started snowing.

We ran together the entire way, each listening to music on our iPods but keeping roughly an eight-minute-mile pace with one another.

At the halfway point, our Garmins beeped at us to turn around. We looked at each other with pride that we were on pace, happy, and enjoying a night run in the snow. We didn't say a word.

We finished just over one hour and forty-five minutes, a few minutes shy of our goal, but exactly when my playlist ended on the last beat of a Wilco song, just in front of his house. It had snowed nearly an inch and a half in the interim.

After cleaning up, we went and ate way too much pizza and drank way too much beer downtown at Poor Richard's. It was there I found out Grant wasn't even training. He hadn't run in ages. He had done that just for me.

It wouldn't be the last time Grant would be there for me. He calls randomly to check in. After he reads my current wife's articles, he follows up with a congratulatory note to us. He occasionally reminisces with me about Lance and U2 or how sad it is that magazines are dying a slow death.

When, thirteen years after our half-snow-marathon, my eldest daughter flew from South Carolina to Colorado to look for a place to move, he graciously picked her up and then lent her his car for the weekend. "Just fill it up with gas," he said, "and we'll call it even."

I have learned more about Jesus from Grant than those who claim to follow him. Every time I fall, he's there to help me up without judgment or questioning. Even though I don't see him often, I'm aware that if I called him this very minute and said, "I can't tell you why, but I need some help. Can you fly here?" Without hesitation, he would do it. He shows that wild reliability the way I imagine Jesus does.

Ever think about how many people wanted to see Jesus as he walked through town? Multitudes of people would hear he was coming, and they'd make plans to see him and ask much of him.

I'm reminded of when Jesus went to help Jairus's daughter, who was incredibly ill. On his way there, he encountered many people who needed him, including the woman who touched his cloak and was healed when Jesus felt the power had left him. In the confusion and crowds, time must've escaped the group, and Jairus's daughter died. Jesus, however, persisted and went to her when others thought it was too late. He told her to "Get up!" and instantly, she stood, healed and healthy.

All God wants from us is a little faith that he will do what he says. That he'll show up when he says. All you need for fuel is your faith. All you need for your kit is the Holy Spirit. And then I imagine him saying, "Let's just call it even."

17 | DAVID BECKHAM

*"Children are the hands by which
we take hold of heaven."*
—Henry Ward Beecher

My daughter, Logan, has always loved soccer and has played since she was not even three years old. She was five when she was introduced to David Beckham, and she instantly idolized his ability to score goals from his free kicks, bending the ball in his trademark fashion.

In January of 2007, news that Beckham had signed a contract to join the Los Angeles Galaxy for the upcoming season after playing for Spain's Real Madrid. Logan, even at six years old, was excited though she didn't know what that meant. I'd tell her, "Well, kiddo, that means he's going to play here in the United States for *our* professional league." That didn't really help. I might as well have been explaining the history of the Ottoman Empire. As the months wore on until his first official Los Angeles game, her excitement grew. That excitement became more palpable when ESPN aired their commercial "Hello, Goodbye," playing The Beatles' song as sad Englanders tore their Beckham posters off their walls while Americans were ramping up to see him.

As we watched the commercial's final clip of Beckham kneeling in the tunnel to tie his Adidas cleats, we both got choked up. That was a big deal for US soccer. Logan was—for all intents and purposes—his number one fan, and I wanted to support her in her soccer crush. When other parents would ask what our kids were into, I would joke that Logan was equally as obsessed with Beckham as she was with Hannah Montana, Miley Cyrus's kids' television character. If she ever saw both of them in the same room, the fear was she would literally rip in half. Choosing between the two wasn't an option. Logan was all girl and all tomboy at the same time.

We were living in Denver, and as luck would have it, this was home to the local Major League Soccer team, Colorado Rapids. They were conveniently in the same division as the Galaxy, so they'd play against each other a few times each year. That first chance was not until August in Commerce City, just outside of Denver, at the new Dick's Sporting Good Park. Becks hadn't debuted in a Galaxy kit until July because he had been nursing a sore ankle, but the excitement was at a fever pitch. I had already bought season tickets for just the two of us near the field, and we had gone to every home game together so far. As that day drew near in August, I surprised her with an official white LA Galaxy Beckham jersey with the number twenty-three on the back, just below his surname. As season ticket holders, we were able to get better seats than our usual seats, and we ended up with ones closer to the field mid-center. I imagined there'd be just a few of us wearing white jerseys among a sea of burgundy.

All day, leading up to the 6:30 p.m. kickoff, she persistently asked how long until we would leave. At 11:00 a.m., "Daddy, when is the game?" Then at 12:10 a.m., "Is it time yet?" On and on, until finally, I decided to head out early, figuring we could hang in the stadium with a soft pretzel and some Cokes until the game started. If we were lucky, maybe we'd see some pre-game practice.

Traffic was awful, as I hadn't anticipated a sold-out game and traffic taking longer than usual. As we rode together, listening to the pregame commentary on the radio, we learned that Beckham's sore ankle might prevent him from playing as it had a few previous games. We still held out hope leading into the night, but then they confirmed Beckham didn't even get on the plane to come. After playing three games on two continents in six days, he was too beat up to travel. She was gutted but still wanted to proceed, even though I could see how sad she was.

When we finally arrived at the stadium, Logan was in awe. She had been with me earlier in the season, but tonight was different. You could feel something in the air. There was this feeling we were going to see something special. That worry about being in the minority while wearing white Galaxy jerseys dissipated as we saw the stadium full of Beckham fans wearing either his number seven jersey from Manchester United, his English National jersey, ones from Real Madrid, or of course, more Galaxy jerseys than Rapids.

After the pregame fanfare, we headed to our special midfield seats with our yellow mustard-covered soft pretzels and readied ourselves. First came the player introductions, and although we *knew* Beckham wasn't there, we were giddy when the Galaxy came out onto the pitch.

We cheered loudly for the Rapids and even louder for the Galaxy. We didn't know why, but we both did.

Then came the booing from the row behind us.

"Go home, Galaxy! Take your lame boy Beckham home, the loser. Beckham, you [sexual slur], go home, you sonofabitch. Damn loser." He was relentless. He was loud, obscene, and obnoxious. For good measure, he dropped a few f-bombs in his insults, too. *Atta boy,* I thought. *Your parents would be proud.* I turned to Logan, and I said, "I'm sorry, kiddo. Don't listen to him." She shrugged it off.

That happened through all the introductions and into a few bars of the national anthem. I had to say something, so I turned around and was about to open my mouth when I saw the largest Hell's Angel-looking man ever. Of course, he was standing on the row behind me, but he still would've been six inches taller had we both been on even ground. Bald, tattooed, and wearing street clothes—no jerseys for him!—he looked down at me and merely said, "What?"

"Just, you know . . . I'm here with my daughter," I said. "Would you mind your language?"

He just looked at me and grunted some words under his breath. I turned back around to view the pitch, nervous now that he was behind me and I couldn't see him.

I looked down to where Logan was standing next to me. I mouthed, "I'm sorry." She smiled. The guy kept going on against Beckham, even though he was back in LA. I was thinking this guy hoped he'd still hear him. "Beckham sucks! Go back to England, you fairy! Bunch of pussies, the Galaxy!"

Without thinking, Logan turned around and pointed her finger at him before I could stop her, and said, "Hey! How would you like it if you loved your sport so much you helped other teams win, only to injure yourself again?" she said while wagging her finger at this man literally five times her size. "Do you think he likes not being here? No! He wanted to be, but he's *hurrrrrtttt!*" She let the word drag on for effect. "You're just . . . you're just a big meanie!"

Logan turned around and went immediately back to cheering without missing a beat, looking at me for approval and taking a bite of her pretzel. She just . . . did what she needed to do.

"I'm sorry, little lady," said the man. He tapped me on the shoulder. I was convinced I was going to get sucker-punched in the face when he simply said, "You have a good kid there." With that, he sat down and didn't say anything the rest of the game unless the Rapids scored, which they did a lot, beating LA three to one.

Support can come from anywhere, I've learned. God has put confidence and gusto into so many people as a gift. My daughter was bold and courageous when I was, frankly, a little frightened. It was my parental duty to say *something*, but to do anything else required something I just lacked inside of me, yet my six-year-old had. Sure, you can say it's innocent, and I'm sure that was part of it, but I learned that while Logan rebuked someone loudly and with courage, she did it kindly.

I wish I had Logan's spirit. She has a quiet intensity about her. She has grit. She has gusto. If you met her in person, you'd love her disposition and kindness—unless you meet her on the soccer pitch, where as a goalkeeper, she takes that ferocity and uses it to intimidate you on the field.

She reminds me of a young David, who courageously—and foolishly?—offered himself up to fight the Philistine giant, Goliath. I imagine his father, Jesse, not to mention all his brothers, feeling the way I had, wondering what would happen next. But God uses all types of people to teach us things, fight for us, and show us how to do it kindly. It's when we see these people in action that we can fully understand what they mean to us and how the Lord uses them. They are, simply, Jesus wrapped in skin.

My daughter is now off to college, where she plays soccer with that same grit. I pray that I have more people in my life with her not-so-silent bravado. It's definitely from Jesus.

18 | MOVENPICK

"The chances you take, the people you meet,
the people you love . . . the faith that you have—that's
what's going to define your life."
—Denzel Washington

The flight from Athens to Cairo wasn't terribly long but was definitely tiring. I had been traveling for over twenty-four hours since leaving Denver, through London then Athens before jumping onto a plane to my final destination in Egypt. I was meeting my old friend from college, Frank, and the two of us were going to cover and document a running race across the Sahara Desert. (When the race director asked me if I knew an adventure photographer, I said yes. Then I immediately called Frank and said, "Hey, do you want to go to Cairo with me?" He agreed, and a week later, he boarded a plane to Cairo but landed hours before me.) I landed at nearly 3:30 a.m. Egyptian time, exhausted.

Though I had traveled internationally quite a bit and sometimes even through Arabic-speaking countries—I was in Dubai covering triathlons in 2005—I was a fish out of water. The Cairo airport was a confusing jumble of languages, with peddlers trying to get tourists to buy anything they were selling—and they were selling a lot. I was walking toward baggage claim when a gentleman came running up to me and said, "American?"

"Yes," I said.

"Tourist!" he exclaimed as if he were guessing an answer on *The $50,000 Pyramid* show. He must have thought my body language was giving him clues "airplane, bags, passport, person, holiday."

"No," I said, "journalist." I had learned long ago to use that as an answer; I would get hassled less in third-world countries. That got him riled up like he was meeting a celebrity.

"Journalist! Journalist! Journalist!" he started exclaiming loudly as he parted the crowd to make way for me to go through customs. He took my arm and led me through this crowd while yelling, "American journalist!" At that point, I wasn't sure what to think. Who was this guy? *Oh, maybe the race sent him to pick me up?* I wondered. He asked for my passport, and I foolishly gave it up. I noted he handed it off to someone who ran off with it. Why was everyone from my plane still waiting in the immigration line and I was getting to pass right through? It didn't seem good. I tried to muster some boldness:

"Hey, no, my passport!"

"It's okay, journalist," said my friend. He patted my chest to reinforce his sincerity.

A minute later, as we're breezing through immigration, his friend returned with my passport, fully stamped with my visa and ready to go. We walked right through immigration, two men handling my bags, through baggage claim, and past customs. No issues. Now I was surrounded by about five Egyptian men, asking me where I was going.

"You want a limousine?" said one.

"No, no. Just a taxi," I said. "You know, a taxi?" I made a steering wheel motion as if that would help.

"Yes, yes, limousine."

"Taxi," I emphatically repeated.

"Okay, okay, where to?"

"Uh . . ." I checked my printed-off paper. "Movenpick Hotel. Media City."

"No Movenpick in Media City." said the one who initially snagged me. They must not have been from the race after all.

"Yes. Movenpick." I repeated.

"Movenpick?" he questioned again.

"Yes. Movenpick."

He called a friend over and asked him something in Arabic, ending with the word Movenpick as a question.

"No Movenpick," said the new guy.

"Yes, Movenpick," I said. It was utterly ridiculous.

"Oh, okay, Movenpick," he said. "Media City?"

I was thinking, *This is like* "Who's on First?" *but in Arabic.*

We finally agreed there was indeed a Movenpick Hotel in Media City and I wanted to go there. Then he begged me to buy a camel ride, a Great Pyramids tour, anything. I finally understood; these guys were hawking their tourist expeditions and saw me as one who had money because of my nationality. I encouraged them all that I might indeed buy a package, but for now, I needed to go to the hotel.

They wanted to confirm one more time, "Movenpick? Media City?"

I was introduced to Ahmed, the limousine driver.

"You need a ride!" he told me, not asking.

"Yes, please," I said.

He took my bags, and we silently marched outside in the predawn hours; we walked past lines of taxis—which was odd, past the terminal—which was scary, past one parking structure—which was unnerving, and then we got to the next parking garage, which looked abandoned and dimly lit—which was terrifying.

"Come," he said, his first word in ten minutes. Then he led me down a ramp to the lower level. There were no cars in sight. I thought to myself, *This is where he's going to kill me.*

As we rounded the corner, there it was: a 1990-something Toyota Camry with patchwork paneling and missing paint. He stood alongside it proudly, dropped my bag, and held up his arms as if he were Vanna White presenting the *Wheel of Fortune* grand prize. "My limousine," he said. He was so proud.

I got into the back seat, assuming that was customary here, too. He revved up his Camry and started to pull away.

We got onto the highway and started to zip away at an ungodly speed without his headlights on. His car's governor started beeping from the excessive speed at anything over 100 kph. We were passing pushcarts, mopeds, and people leading camels by makeshift reins. Then, to cut across town, we turned against traffic and started passing cars *going the other direction.* All that without the Camry's headlights on.

"Lights?" I begged from the back seat.

"Burns petrol," said Ahmed, meaning that the lights would burn gas.

"Uh, I don't think it works that way. Lights!"

"Petrol, petrol! Not good. Burns petrol."

Okay, I am definitely dying today.

Just then, during my terror, he turned around to ask, "Do you like English music?"

"Yeah, I do," I said, assuming he meant British music. Half

expecting The Clash to play from his speakers, it was actually "Kim," from Eminem. I turned his volume a half-turn to the right, and his digital CD player's blue neon lights spun up to the noise level 86. He started singing.

> *Don't you get it, bitch? No one can hear you!*
> *Now shut the fuck up and get what's comin' to you!*
> *You were supposed to love me!*
> *Now bleed, bitch, bleed! Bleed, Bleed, Bitch! Bleed!*

It was insane. Ahmed had no idea he was singing about Eminem killing his wife, but he knew every single word. Every one! There we were, speeding down the wrong side of the highway, with Eminem blaring so loudly, struggling to drown out the governor's incessant and unsyncopated beeping, dodging people and camels at 5:00 a.m.

"I *love* English music," Ahmed screamed over this cacophony. For an hour solid, he proceeded to sing every lyric of that album until we reached the hotel. Man, was I glad to see Frank.

I was in a strange place and didn't speak the language. I was lost in a sea of miscommunication and cultural differences. They looked at me and thought that because I was American, I had money. I looked at them and thought they were backward and third-world. We were both wrong.

I was walking alone in the world, even though I had a few friends—none of them knew the real me or my struggles. I looked at them, people like Frank, with jealousy. Frank might as well have Henry David Thoreau's quotation that "all good things are wild and free" tattooed on his chest. He loved people, and he longed for travel. It had been since the days of building a badminton court in the backyard, Frank just showed up in any circumstance.

I had called him just a week before the trip and said, "Do you want to go to the Sahara Desert with me?"

"Yes," he said. He was wild that way. He was also free. The details of taking off work and getting a plane ticket were minor to him. He just came, unabashed and excited to be in a new land with an old friend and experience something different.

My connection with the Lord was slipping away, and it was definitely showing itself by my lack of kindness and acceptance for others. I hadn't read the scriptures in ages, and I didn't have a North Star to guide me in my life. While Frank, and people like him, were free and running, they had purpose. I was flailing and running around wildly without direction, hardly an ambassador to Christ. Hardly a believer.

Ahmed eventually found the Movenpick—yes, it was in Media City—even though he circled the massive compound many times before deciding it was truly the place, confirmed when he finally turned on his car lights which shined brightly onto the monument with the word Movenpick on it. We pulled into the hotel's roundabout. It was quiet and still outside, still quite early in the morning. He barely turned down his radio to turn around, say goodbye, and shake my hand—but at least the beeping had stopped. I had paid his friends back at the airport for the ride, so all that was left was to grab my bags and open the door. Maybe I paused because I was tired. Maybe it was because I still felt a little scared of my surroundings. But at that moment, Ahmed looked me in the eye and smiled, then said in his broken English as he shook my hand, "Goodbye, my friend." He meant it.

As he zoomed away in his limousine, I could hear the stereo come back up to full volume, getting louder the farther he went. Eminem continued singing, and I could imagine Ahmed singing aloud with him in his little Camry.

Hmm, I thought. Maybe a stranger can feel at home if home goes with him wherever he goes.

Then I saw his lights go off.
They burn petrol, after all.

19 | RUNNING THE ROCKIES

"Survey the path for your feet,
and all your ways will be sure."
—Proverbs 4:26

Each autumn, nearly two hundred crazy ultrarunners line up in Buena Vista, Colorado, for the start of the TransRockies Run, a 6-day, 120-mile stage race through the Rocky Mountains, ending in Beaver Creek, a few peaks over to the west. In 2009, I was one of the crazy ones.

A friend of mine who I had met running in the Sahara Desert, Matt, was a retired major in the US Marine Corp, and although a little goofy, he was tough as nails. For instance, during that 2007 Sahara Race, he was hit by a truck during the last stage into Giza— the only city stage—with six miles to go. He ran with a broken arm to the finish line before accepting medical attention.

Matt had convinced me that although I only ran about 40 of the 200-something miles of that Sahara race, I could handle running all of the 120 miles in the Rockies. I thought so, too, and I decided to toe the line with him.

Now, here's the thing about *this* race: It is a team race, with two partners teaming up together to tackle the whole thing. You both run every mile together, and although passing through multiple checkpoints each day, you cannot pass through them more than two minutes apart from each other—time penalties or disqualification can occur. You are only as fast as your slowest person, so it benefited us to help each other, unselfishly, to get us both to the finish line. If one could run nine-minute miles and one only eleven-minute miles, you would both be running elevens. If you thought about going faster, you would have to wait before you got to the checkpoint and risk cramping by stopping so abruptly.

We had decided to run together.

Matt came from South Florida, which was at sea level. The race started in Buena Vista, Colorado, at 7,900 feet, and more than 50% of the time, we'd be above 9,000 feet. A daunting task if you're coming from Denver, as I was, but it was downright stupid to come from Florida, and Matt knew it. So, he slept in an oxygen chamber for three months leading up to the race, reducing the amount of oxygen in his "bubble" to mimic the thin air of the Rockies.

It didn't help.

On the first day of running, through the high desert of what the locals call "BV," neither one of us was prepared. It was sandy, hot, and dry. Blisters on our feet were common. Friction burns from our packs were eating the skin off the smalls of our backs. A misplaced water bottle hanging from my chest strap was unknowingly wearing a hole near my armpit, which blistered and opened, causing a stinging pain that felt like someone had put lemon juice in a paper cut.

Lucky for us, the first stage leveled most of the teams. The leaders came in around three hours. We came into town with a bunch of other teams mid-pack, about an hour and a half back from the leaders.

Day two was looming. With a 6:30 a.m. start time (all

the teams started together each day in mass start—think Tour de France-style), we didn't have enough time to rest, get massages, and charge our Garmins, but we had no choice. We showed up to the start line about a minute before the gun went . . .

. . . off!

We started running up a gently climbing gravel road into the forest on a Jeep trail before turning onto the single-track Continental Divide Trail. There, we ran up what felt like the side of a building for two-and-a-half miles to the 12,500-foot summit of Hope Pass. The only problem: the single-track trail looked like a scene of climbers heading up Everest's Hillary Step during the busy season because it was littered with slow runners and walkers humbled by the steep terrain. I got impatient and shuffled around the walkers and slowpokes to run up ahead, doing the miles solo. I was flying and felt great. Unbeknownst to me, Matt, however, had a crushing sensation on his chest and began walking with the older runners. I didn't slow down until I reached the summit. Then I waited for him to catch up.

Ten minutes. Twenty minutes. Thirty minutes passed. On the top of the pass, the winds kicked up, and I got cold. First, I pulled out a jacket, then a beanie, then gloves. I had left Matt so far behind that standing around waiting was turning me hypothermic, my core getting cold as my sweat was cooling me down too quickly. By the time he caught me—I was a mess. Luckily, the checkpoint was down the other side and not at the top.

Eventually, I warmed up, took some energy gels, and launched into a downward run with Matt. We were far behind, so we added some speed as best we could down a pine-needle trail, much softer and cushier than the pea gravel on the ascent, enabling us to try to make up time. If we averaged sixteen-minute miles up the mountain, we easily halved that coming down. We pulled into the finish line without losing more time, which for the day was a win.

On the third day, it was more of the same, me feeling great, and Matt feeling awful—the altitude really getting to him. My frustration with him was at a boiling point, but I kept my cool and soldiered on, albeit at a slow, twelve-minute-per-mile pace.

The day was nearly a marathon in length and had steep climbs and descents before entering Camp Hale, the old World War II-era Army Base where they trained Nordic soldiers for war in the Alps. We pulled into camp for the day, losing another hour on the leaders.

I was mad. And exhausted, which isn't a good combination, so I ate dinner and closed my eyes in our tent early, trying not to look Matt in the eye. *Did you even train for this?* I wondered.

On the morning of day four, I woke up to find Matt already up and about, packed, and geared up for the day. He had already eaten breakfast and was raring to go. I was able to quickly follow suit and ready myself for the day, but something was off. My head was in a fog, and I was slightly dizzy. My stomach was upset, and I feared I had caught something.

I ate a bit of food in hopes of settling my stomach, and we set off for the day, a fifteen-mile slog through various terrain and down a trail filled with creek water, which followed the same path.

From the first mile, I knew I was off. My pace slowed, and I drifted behind Matt, who seemed to have super-speed. When we got to the peak of the climb, at mile six, we reached 11,600 feet. I had to rest. I had no energy, no will. I was spent.

"C'mon, Kyle. You got this. Flat for three miles, then downhill to camp!" Matt yelled.

"Yeah," I said, defeated.

"You got this. Let's go!"

He walked back to me, lifted me up from a rock, and looked me in the eye. "You. Got. This," he said from an inch away from my face. "Let's go."

More to save face than to rise to the challenge, I followed his orders and got up. The next three miles were painful and slow. When we hit the downhill, I told him to keep going and just hold up when he hit the next checkpoint. He wouldn't have it. He stayed with me.

Why is he doing this? I hadn't waited for him. I hadn't encouraged him. And now, I was the lowest common denominator. My speed meant his speed, and he didn't complain in the least.

Paul said in Corinthians not to be unevenly yoked, in a marriage, as partners. I wasn't planning on marrying Matt, but we were in this together. I was weak, and he was strong. While I was running my race the last three days, Matt was running *our* race, together. He not only never let two minutes come between us, but he also never let two feet come between us. *Is this what a partnership is?*

The rest of the day was a mixture of silence from me and encouragement from Matt. We stumbled into camp late, again. We lost another thirty minutes and were in last place in our division.

The penultimate stage was more of the same, but over twenty-four long miles, the first ten of which were uphill again from our 8,500-foot tent city to over 11,500 feet. Matt had yelled, "You got this!" so many times that when I think of that day, that's all I hear in my head. He slowed for me, again, and at some points, was humbled down to a walk. I was done.

"You are not finished, Kyle," he said. "You trained for this; you're mentally prepared. You're faster than I am. Now get your ass up and run!"

It was like this most of the day, and by the time we hit the downhill, a short, six-mile rapid descent, we got into a rhythm—faster than earlier in the day, but slower than my pace back at normal elevation. By days' end, we had clawed back the time we had lost from the last two days. When we crossed the line together, onlookers would've thought we had won the whole thing. We high-fived, hugged, slapped each other on the back, and smiled the biggest smiles we had all week. We ate our meal together in the big tent and then went back to our tent to plan the strategy for day six—something we hadn't done before.

The course was twenty-two miles the next day, doing a counterclockwise semicircle from Vail to Beaver Creek. The elevation never surpassed 10,500 feet, and the climbs were intermittent and easier grades than previously.

We decided to run the first eleven hard—as hard as we could—in hopes of passing some teams that were letting up a bit. We'd then rest at the top at a slow jog as we refueled, then attack the descent with a fury.

We agreed, shook on it, and lined up on the line, that time toward the front.

That day flew by. We traded positions to fight the wind and kept the same pace all morning, matching each other's cadence, too. Each time our feet hit the dirt trail, they were in unison. We started passing teams at an unreal clip uphill, at just under nine-minute miles. They didn't give chase because we were so far behind on the leaderboard, which only fueled our plan.

At the top, we slowed to a walk, changed water bottles from our packs to our chests, scarfed down some gels and energy chews, and picked up the pace, even faster this time.

We were relentless. We didn't stop again for anything.

When we arrived in Beaver Creek, after running down a ski run, we crossed the line again together. There was not much fanfare—no one came to watch these things. But we celebrated in the cabin, showered up and put on street clothes, and went to dinner, where we mingled and chatted with the other teams.

"What happened to you guys?" people asked. "We didn't see you at all today."

Matt and I smiled. "We found our gas," said Matt. "So we hit the pedal."

Overall, we still fared poorly in the scheme of the race. But

I learned so many valuable lessons. When I felt good, I took off, leaving Matt to fend for himself. But when I was struggling, he did no such thing. He not only waited and stayed with me, but he matched my pace and even encouraged me to go on.

I hadn't had many Matts in my life like that. I thought I had to run the race myself, damn the others. I thought I had to muster my own strength and not lean on those with me. Even worse, I thought when I was the one with strength—it'd be a one-man show.

I was wrong. The life race I was running was not meant to be run solo. I needed to slow down and consider my fellow racers, and I needed encouragement and accountability myself. I hadn't ever had that. Not from my parents, not from my friends, and not from any partner I'd ever had.

That only served to embolden my anger toward God and the world. *If I didn't have a partner, then I'd do it myself,* I thought.

I couldn't have been more wrong, but I also couldn't hear him in the midst of running solo.

20 | SAY AGAIN?
*"I hadn't really noticed that I had a hearing problem.
I just thought most people had given
up on speaking clearly."*
—Hal Linden

I would make fun of my brother because he was eleven years older than me. I would tell him, "When you're fifty, I'll still be in my thirties." I'd tease him for his hearing, getting older, and dealing with back issues. It was my way of getting back at him for teasing me as a child. He would routinely lay in waiting outside the stair's railing as I barreled down the steps from my bedroom, then he'd pop his hand through spindles covered in an old wizard puppet, giving it a creepy, high-pitched voice. I'd pee myself and either turn around and cry for our mother or run down and cry for our mother. I was six. He was seventeen. So, I figured I could make fun of his growing waistline and hearing issues all I wanted. I had the right, so to speak.

When I started developing a hearing issue, I didn't want to tell him. I didn't realize I was having trouble hearing at all until people pointed it out. They would ask me questions, and I wouldn't hear what they had said. Then I started noticing it myself shortly afterward. It was mostly in restaurants, bars, or even at the gym. When people were talking to me, I found myself asking, "Huh? What did you say? Say again?"

It was starting to get pretty old, being with my friends or family and not being able to hear a word. I noticed that on certain days, I had to turn up the TV volume, yet on other days, not at all. I was starting to get pretty upset not understanding the pattern, but more importantly, at thirty-something years old, I was wondering why in the heck I couldn't hear. I felt I was too young to lose my hearing.

I reluctantly called my brother and mentioned it. He had said he, too, had a hearing problem and reminded me that our grandmother used to say she had very small ear canals—and that was why she couldn't hear. He encouraged me to go to the doctor. Maybe I had small ear canals, too?

Without health insurance at the time, I decided to visit a hearing aid store instead of a physician. It was a free consultation, so I figured, *Why not?* They gave me the routine test, and the results were undeniable: I needed hearing aids. They showed me some options, starting at $2,500—but told me not to worry as I could use a payment plan.

I went to about three or four of these types of places, and each one had the same story. I would check in, they would give me a fancy test, and—Wouldn't you know it?—the results were always the same: I needed hearing aids. While the cost varied from store to store, it could be anywhere from $2,500–$5,000. But hey, if I ordered them *today*, I could get twenty percent off.

After some research and finally biting the bullet and talking to a physician, I was able to book an appointment with his referral to the Hearing Specialty Center at the University of Colorado in Denver.

I went in one morning on the way to work, and right away, something was different from the hearing aid stores. There were no hearing aids on display or for sale in the lobby; they asked me to describe what I could hear versus merely measuring what I couldn't hear; they asked me if there were any differences between when I couldn't hear versus when I could, and they gave me a much more scientific and foolproof test.

When the technician came out after my test, the results were decisive once again, but instead of proving that I *couldn't* hear, the test proved with 100% certainty that I *could*. I had perfect hearing. I wondered, *Had those hearing aid stores been scamming me?* Yet, I also knew I had trouble hearing.

The technician asked me to put the headphones back on, then went into her little booth and proceeded to give me the exact same hearing test again. This time, however, she introduced other noises, too: low, mid-range, and high-frequency sounds. Then, she introduced other sounds and background noises. First, the ones similar to a coffee shop, with its clinks and conversations, spoons hitting the sides of ceramic mugs, and the occasional chatter. Then it was low air-conditioning hums, the kind that sounds like white noise and drowns out anything else. Other common sounds came next: the noise you'd hear in a room full of children, a small concert setting, and an office party.

That time, the results were drastically different. The mid and high frequencies didn't affect my hearing, but the low ones did. I couldn't hear at all. She concluded that if there was a low hum or rumble from things like crowd noise, a dishwasher, or an air conditioner in the background, I was unable to hear normal voices well. It was the introduction of these foreign noises that were clouding my brain's ability to distinguish. The good news was I did not need hearing aids, but the bad news was that I did have a hearing problem and I needed a plan to address it.

I would need to be better prepared when going out to dinner with friends or family. I tried to avoid busier, louder restaurants to ensure I was part of the conversation. I didn't want to be the one to say, "Say again?" every two minutes. During that time, it wasn't just low-frequency sounds that were drowning out the voices around me: a new car, new home, better job, a raise, travel, exercise—all to stay out of the house)—all of that *stuff* became low-frequency "noise" in my life, and I couldn't hear anything, nor anyone else. God's voice was inaudible to me. I'm sure he didn't stop speaking to me; I just couldn't hear him anymore. Some of it was deliberate. *Why would I want to listen to God anyway?* I wasn't sure I wanted to hear him if I could.

And I don't think God shouted over all that noise. I think he was waiting patiently for me to quiet my life noise so he could whisper. In 1 Kings 19, he speaks to Elijah not in the wind, an earthquake, nor a fire, but in a gentle whisper. I had to calm my life to hear him, but I hadn't . . . yet.

I never got hearing aids. My hearing in these circumstances has worsened, and now I strain and focus to hear dinner conversation at a loud restaurant. My impairment doesn't stop my friends and family from trying to speak to me, and thankfully, neither does my spiritual impairment stop the Lord.

21 | CROWING ROOSTER
"But whoever denies me before men, I also will deny before my Father who is in heaven."
—Jesus, Matthew 27:33

On our second or third date, not too far into seeing other that it would matter, but as I dropped off my date at her house that evening, we merely said goodbye in our seats—there was no walking to the door tonight.

During our small goodbye talk, the radio station had an advertisement for a local church.

The commercial said, "Ever wonder about where you came from? About God in the universe, or why you long for a better life? Have you given any thought to Jesus Christ? Come every Sunday to—"

"Jesus?" she said. "What a joke."

"I'm sorry?" I said, wondering what that meant. I hadn't been going to church in a long time, and I couldn't recall the last time I had even prayed, but I still believed this guy was real.

"Jesus," she repeated. "What a bunch of bullshit."

"What, you don't think he's real?"

"He's not," she said.

"Okay, wait a second," I blurted out, turning my whole body toward her in the passenger seat. "You may not believe he was the Son of God, but he was most certainly real."

"I disagree," she said adamantly.

"But, I don't understand," I continued. "He's been proven factually to have existed. He's in the historical record. Both Josephus and the Romans have documents backing up his existence as well as the disciples. He was real."

"Can we agree to disagree?" she said and grabbed the door handle to get out.

"Whoa, whoa, whoa, hold on a second."

"What?" she said casually as if she had forgotten we were talking about this.

"Okay, let's say you don't believe he existed."

"Right, that's what I'm saying."

"The disciples? The apostles? You know the twelve guys who followed him anywhere he went?"

"So, what's your point?"

"*Those* guys wrote the Bible! Part of it anyway. There's no dispute they existed."

"Great. So again, what's your point?"

"Oh, so these guys were real, right? It's documented that they were all killed. Why would they write about their own doubt in the Bible?"

"I don't know, why?" she said sarcastically.

"Because it happened!" I said. "Then, what happened later in their lives that got them to come out of hiding and not only be seen but to preach what they saw? These guys ran and hid when they arrested Jesus, a person. They feared they would be next, so they cowered together, afraid. Yet next we hear of them, they were preaching boisterously to anyone and everyone that Jesus was Lord. Something happened in-between."

"They were crazy."

"Nope, I don't buy that. They saw something. They experienced something. It was the resurrection. They saw Jesus alive. It's the only thing that makes sense."

"Sure it does," she said under her breath, sarcasm thick as honey.

"If tomorrow someone said to you, with a gun to your head, tell me you never knew Kyle or we'll kill you, what would you do?"

"I'd say I didn't know you."

"Right," I said, getting more agitated. "Now, what if you had seen me do something so miraculous, so crazy, so . . . otherworldly that you felt like that experience was bigger than you, bigger than death?"

She didn't say anything.

"You'd be like, 'Go ahead and kill me. I don't know what I saw, but I know that it's bigger than whatever you can do to me.'"

"Yeah, maybe."

"Maybe?" I went on. "These guys died horrific deaths because they wouldn't disavow even knowing Jesus. And it was a lot more painful and slow than a bullet to the head: spear thrusts, a bag of snakes tied around their head, burned alive, stoned to death, beheaded, and crucified upside down. They died because Jesus died for us."

There was a long, uncomfortable pause.

"You don't actually believe any of that stuff." She laughed. "Do you?"

I didn't know what to think. Say yes, and there goes my date. Say no and . . . well, what was the harm in that?

"No. Of course not."

I ended up marrying that woman in the car in the fall of 2009. Partially because I felt no one else would want me. Partially because I felt I was a bit better than her, and therefore she'd never leave, which, in hindsight, wasn't only unfair, but a pitiful, shameful reason to be with someone. We soon found ourselves in a typical "roommate marriage," wherein if you replaced one of us with a roommate, the other would hardly skip a beat—as long as they paid rent.

We moved to California to chase her dream job two months after we wed. I went, knowing finding a job would be difficult but moved, regardless. Within two weeks of being in California, we started going to marriage counseling. It was my idea. We weren't talking at all, and something needed to change. I found a counselor nearby on Piedmont Avenue and scheduled an appointment. On the first trip, we sat on either end of the sofa. At the end of that session, the therapist asked if we would split up and come separately. She would be first. After that one session, she came home, slammed the door, opened a bottle of Two Buck Chuck, and promptly said, "Well, clearly you're the one with the issues. I'm never going back."

We knew it was a mistake to be married, and everything was suffering. When my daughter would visit, we'd be alone. I'd pick her up from the airport by myself, spend time alone with her, and take her everywhere. I would find out much later that she had asked my sister, "Why does Daddy's wife hate me?" It was heartbreaking.

But it was also something to be covered up. I couldn't fail at this, as miserable as I was, and admitting I was unhappy was sinful in my secular world. So I bucked up, found a great job, moved up the ladder, and never looked back. I returned to the same comfort that I had when I was a child: my bike and triathlons. I'd swim in Aquatic Park, run down the Embarcadero, and ride up Redwood Road into the obscure trails high in the Oakland hills. It felt like my only freedom was being outside for hours.

Together, we ended up having two amazing children, Jackson and Morgan, born exactly two years apart, who in their own right were wonderful distractions.

She stopped working to care for the kids, and I continued my career—never going back to the Lord for anything. I certainly didn't step foot in a church. Not for a wedding, not a funeral, not for a bake sale. Christianity was verboten in our house, and I happily fell in line. My Bible was gathering dust in an attic somewhere. I never brought up my faith or Jesus again.

Weekends and summer mornings before work, I would spend on long rides alone. Any time I could be out of the house (or apart), I would take it—with that maneuver, I didn't have to face anything, most of all my own mortality, unhappiness, or worse.

From the outside, my Instagram life looked perfect: a beautiful house, two kids from this marriage—plus my older daughter—a few paid-off cars, and vacations.

But I was hiding it all from people. According to my Strava app, where I log my mileage for running and cycling, I rode over 4,200 miles in 2016 and 3,000 in 2017.

Then, once after a long ride, I was at West End Bikes in downtown Portland and I thought I recognized a familiar face.

"Josh?" I said.

The man turned around; I immediately knew I had made the right call.

"Kyle?"

"Holy shit, man," I said, and I just hugged him out of desperation, I think, because I hadn't hugged a man in a decade. I hadn't seen Josh since outside the coffee shop in Boulder, and we had lost touch again.

"What are you doing here?" he said.

"I live here in Portland. You?"

"Same," he said excitedly. "Well, actually Lake Oswego, so not far."

"It's so good to see you," I said. "We need to get together."

"Oh, absolutely," he said. "We're going to have to make up for lost time."

"Damn straight," I replied. *Who says damn straight anymore?*

"Let's race on Tuesday at PIR."

"PIR?" I asked.

"The raceway. Portland International Raceway."

"Is it a velodrome?" I asked.

"No, they race cars there. But on Tuesday nights, they open it up for road racing. You need to come."

"I'm in," I said, knowing I would be out of my league. I hadn't raced in years, so I'd be starting over, in Category 5, the beginners. He was a Cat 3.

We exchanged numbers, and I went back to the office across the street. I couldn't believe Josh was in town.

We raced Tuesdays, we had coffees, we had beers, and we rode a lot in between. We caught up often and texted even more so. But one day, he broke the news to me that although he had lived in Portland for nearly a decade, he had promised his wife that at a certain point, they would move back to her home state of Michigan. That time had come, and he was moving in a few weeks to Ann Arbor with his wife and three girls.

Now I can't say I knew him well, but he had been a friend since those days on our bikes and skateboards in Allentown. Why would he keep popping into my life here and there? He was just as kind, giving, and warm as I had always remembered. I recently learned that while he was raised Jewish from his dad's side, his wife is an evangelical Christian.

God was chasing me. And he was starting to get through.

22 | OVER A PINT
*"Arrogance and self-awareness
seldom go hand-in-hand."*
—M to James Bond, *Casino Royale*

I was nervous as all get out when he tapped me on my shoulder that day in April 2015. Steve Murray wasn't very tall, but he was intimidating. As the new CEO of Dr. Martens, he wanted to meet the guy that one of his global vice presidents had hired over in the US. So, he set up a meeting with me on my first day in London, with my full jetlag being evident.

I was scared to death. I didn't want him to know that years prior, I was fired suddenly from KEEN because the owner and I didn't see eye to eye and I wouldn't back down. When he got to that part of my resume, he just said, "Wow, you lasted there longer than most." I was relieved.

Steve—he insisted I called him that—was originally from Scotland, but had lived in the US for decades, first while serving as the brand president of Vans, then as the president of Urban Outfitters. He was back in the UK, with an accent that had been influenced by years abroad.

We talked about the importance of bringing the brand back to life and the way we'd do it. He loved a few things in life: turning around businesses was high on his list. The Premier League and a good pint—in which we had our fair share together over the years—were the others. He would ask me over our two and a half years working together about my opinion on topics that ranged from design to advertising campaigns, new product lines, or even retail expansion. That meant a lot to me.

When we parted ways that first day, I was half-relieved that he didn't fire me on day one, and I can only assume that he was relieved to leave our conversation with the only American standing in the Camden office of Docs.

He hadn't hired the woman who had hired me. That would have been the former CEO just before the board hired Steve to replace him. Steve was candid that he didn't know much about e-commerce, the skill for which I was hired, or this whole new digital landscape. For years, he was busy building more Vans retail stores and growing them to a $1 billion evaluation. You know, easy stuff.

My official title was the vice president of e-commerce, US. My role was newly created to help grow the US region of our online presence. Though I knew this stuff inside and out, having previously grown the e-commerce channels for Speck Products, Nau, Chrome Industries, and KEEN Footwear, there was never a time I didn't feel like an imposter. Steve didn't know what he didn't know, but he trusted me to build the biggest region of the company outside of the United Kingdom. Could I do it? Sometimes I felt like yes, sometimes no.

"Look at this," he said about six months into my tenure, both of us half-drunk on British lager, having dinner in an Indian restaurant in North London, drawing a triangle on the back of his vindaloo-stained napkin. "This was me, at the top of Vans," he said, pointing to the top of the pyramid. Then he drew several horizontal lines to fill the triangle.

"Is this the USDA Food Pyramid?" I asked, half-joking at my own American humor. I can only handle a beer or two.

Steve looked up. "No," he simply said sternly before going back to his scribbling. "Look here, this second row? These were all my lieutenants," pronouncing it *leff-tenants*. "Now? All vice presidents of some sort within the VF Group," he said, name dropping the parent company, which also owns Icebreaker, The North Face, Timberland, Wrangler, and many more.

He pointed to the third row. "These guys? They're now presidents of other brands like Quicksilver."

"They all worked for you?" I asked.

"Dooferd," he mispronounced. "This is you," he said, stabbing his finger into a glob of saag paneer near his pyramid, slightly near that third row of people. "This is you . . . *now*. The president gig will come."

I was struck a bit dumbfounded. "Now?"

"Stick with me. Do as your told. Keep bringing your brilliance to Docs, and let's sell some fucking boots," he said. Then, like a true Scot, he grabbed his pint glass and downed the last bit of his frothy nectar, slammed it onto the table, and wiped the little remnants of liquid from his mouth on the back of his right hand. *Note to self: CEOs can be dramatic, but it works.* I was in.

There was something about me that Steve liked, and no matter what I thought I was, I was going to fall in line. Maybe it was the confidence oozing from the persona I had created. Maybe I reminded him of Doug Palladini, Mitch Whitaker, or Dana Guidice, the men who had helped him run Vans into the stratosphere, who all were in that pyramid somewhere. Maybe I was just . . . good?

I was in London so much that I soon tired of the Holiday Inn on Jamestown Road, the old standby for all traveling employees, and snagged an apartment at the corner of Jamestown and Oval Roads in the same Camden neighborhood of London, overlooking the Grand Union Canal, which people just called "The Canal." Each morning—eight hours ahead of my home in Portland—I had a ritual: run The Canal for a 5K or bike around nearby Regent's Park for a few laps with local roadies, get coffee at the corner shop, work a full day, and grab a pint at the pub afterward, usually with Steve, if he was in town. Apart from long rides on the occasional weekend I was there, I never left Camden or anything more than ten blocks in any direction from my little British flat.

Soon after our pyramid talk, my boss was let go for botching the relaunch of the global website, and when my small US team came to the rescue to salvage the business online, I was called to be the interim global vice president. When we ultimately succeeded, proving our mettle and not that it was a fluke, I was given the role permanently—and with it came a seat at the big boys' table, a spot on the senior executive leadership team. I would sit along with the presidents of each of the three regions and the heads of product, sourcing, legal, and HR—all of us flanking Steve and the CFO around the boardroom.

That was awkward. Out of the nine of us, I was the youngest one in the room by a decade, the only American, and the only one who didn't wear a collared shirt to work. "Don't worry," said Steve, "It's more like a Dr. Martens rebel to dress your way." I agreed. Once, at a leadership retreat in Bath, England, I came to breakfast in a white T-shirt, blue jeans, and bare feet; I was teased relentlessly, never to live it down. "I said the black tee and black jeans were rebellious," he said, "not this American shit."

In one of the first executive meetings I attended, Steve introduced my addition to the team and then went on a diatribe to explain how the nine of us would change the course of this business for the better. He went around the room to say something about each person—"Darren, you're the best product guy there is," he said, looking at the head of product formerly from Asics. "Dan, you're growing Europe," to the EMEA president, and so on until he got to me. "*Dooferd* . . . you have . . . really girly tattoos," he said, laughing loudly about the hibiscus flowers on my forearm before he went on to others. I got what he was doing, showing the others that we were friendly with each other and that we had a good relationship, but the opposite happened. Not only was the impact on my psyche largely negative, but it didn't help my stature among my colleagues. *Was I only here because my "rebellious self-expression" was more on-brand than the legal team's department head?* I wondered.

When it came time to announce some major news about the business, Steve would always ring me up in Portland or tag me when I came to London, which was increasingly more necessary with my new global role. I was the only executive team member not living full time in London, but wherever he found me, he would start immediately after I answered, "Hello?"

"Dooferd, what do you think of . . ." and ask me a myriad of questions. He didn't need my answer; I later would find out, he just wanted to know how my mind thought so that if ever I was called upon to help from the bench, he knew he could count on me. He was grooming me for a bigger role.

Over a pint one night, we started talking about our families: how my relationship with my wife was strained and hard, but man, my kids were amazing. His kids, now grown and ending high school, he and his wife were able to spend more quality time together when he was in town.

"Marriage is hard," he said, "but worth it."

I agreed to disagree.

Within two years of being hired, I was cooking with gas.

We had gone from exactly one person on the e-commerce team in America to nearly fifty-eight globally. We launched new websites localized in languages across Europe, Japan, and Korea. We opened up the Chinese market. I helped drive the marketing through online offerings and brand ideas. We opened distribution centers, created new warranty and returns processes, and I even added thoughts to the product team when asked. My salary had ballooned, my travel budget was extraordinary, and I looked forward to my time alone in that tiny Camden flat, with just a bike in the corner waiting for me to come back every three weeks or so for a ride around the park and to "work my arse off," as they'd say.

The faith Steve and other leaders had in me—and the risk they took on me—paid off. But the price I would end up paying was too much. After two years of travel, sixty-hour work weeks, and late-night calls to Japan or early morning calls to London, I was exhausted. I needed a break from life, from work, and from my wife. I didn't know how to make that happen without disappointing so many people that I failed to make a decision at all—I avoided it all and just kept working harder.

While Steve had a penchant for promoting me—he would again promote me to also oversee a new digital lab, lightly based on the Nike Digital Lab in Oregon—it was his CFO, John, who was constantly asking me to make more money, get more margin, or add a few more growth points to my next year's budget numbers. Once, during budget season, he even said the words to me, "I had no idea how we'd hit the board's expectations, then I just figured you'd find it somewhere like you always do!" From a need to please and to feel valued, I said, "Yes, I will," and I said that often. As a consequence, we grew our channel astronomically, but a side effect was poor mental health. I was cracking. I mustered on because, as John had told me in so many words, "Let's grow this thing, make a ton of cash, exit, and do it again."

When I mentioned my decreasing appetite for extra workload and travel for the first time to Steve, he brushed me off. I hadn't known it yet, but he was facing his own struggle with the board, which ended in his retirement from the company in the fall of 2017. I was no longer protected and knew the writing was on the wall for me, too. The chairman, a former grocery store CEO, and the one who butted heads with Steve, wanted his core executive team in London and didn't necessarily want a T-shirt-wearing, tattooed American who ran a channel he didn't fully understand on his team.

My days were numbered.

I started to lose it. So much that the head of HR sent me an executive coach to help me understand the balance of business and life. I began to pray again, but much like I was praying as a child, wanting to be magically transported out of my home and into the back of the General Lee, I didn't know to what I was praying. I hadn't even *thought* about Jesus in years—he had been once again relegated to a curse word—my mother would not have been pleased, had I been speaking to her—but I was praying to something.

That was when they brought that coach to me, Sam.

Sam lived in Portland, was relaxed, caring, and kind. Within seconds of his walking into my office, I recognized that kind of demeanor: Mike, my old Young Life leader from twenty-five years earlier, was the same. I don't know what possessed me to say anything to him about it, but out it came. "You remind me of my old Young Life leader from high school," I said.

Sam smiled. "Yeah? I know Young Life well. I'm a Christian."

Uh-oh, I thought, how am I going to play this one?

"I used to be," I said. "Er . . . I am one? Hell—I mean *heck*—I don't know."

"That's okay," said Sam. "You don't have to. He does."

We talked about goals and life, and I told him about my unraveling marriage, exhaustion, and declining performance.

"You're trying to run ten marathons at once," he said. "Now, other coaches may tell you to stop doing them. But I'm going to tell you to just do one or two of them—hard."

"What?" I asked. "You want me to go harder? I'm falling apart."

"Strategically," said Sam. "Look, you were made with gifts, so show them off and do something great with them—delegate the rest."

"Okay . . . ?"

"You've been doing marathons. But you're a fixer. You're built for sprints. Fix something, hard and fast. Then relax before you tackle the next one. I'm telling you not to slow down but to hit the accelerator on the *right* things."

That was the day Sam started praying for me. Just not out loud and not with me in the room.

I was meeting with Sam once a month, and while his companionship was comforting, I was starting to break. With Steve gone, I felt like every move I made was in error. Although business was growing, part of our arrangement was that the local teams in each market would report directly to their regional president and eliminate a global team that reported to me.

My new digital team oversaw best practices but had little to no authority to enforce anything locally, given we were sometimes running counter to the will of the market president. As a result, we were left exposed. The interim CEO didn't want to fund the "pet project" of a lab, and we were left scratching our heads, literally having worked ourselves out of a job.

I was becoming neurotic about answering the phone at all times of day or night, fearing it was the board. I started making dumb decisions, and—instead of focusing on what I knew best, e-commerce—I doubled down on the lab concept, moved offices, and holed up on the sixth floor of our Portland offices, trying to create something so extraordinary that the board would love us, er . . . me. Inadvertently by doing so, I took my eye off the prize of the company: the growing online department. I was showing them it still grew without me thinking about it at all. Even the CFO, John, started to realize the tool we had built was self-satisfying. It wasn't me that made them money; it was the machine we had created.

I was holding on for dear life but wasn't even sure what I was holding.

23 | YES MAN

"Say 'Yes,' and you'll figure it out afterward."
—Tina Fey

M y life had looked good from the outside: a job as the global senior vice-president for an international brand, a large house, a few cars, and enough vacation time to not know how to use it. I flew everywhere first-class, drank single malt Glenfiddich Scotch—neat, mind you, never with rocks—made more annually than I ever had, and quite often gave talks to crowds of five hundred business leaders or more. I lived the perfect Instagrammable life and lived up to that label, posting pictures from all vantage points of that life: atop luxury high-rise rentals, from seat 1A in a jumbo sky-liner, or riding a $12,000 bicycle across Europe. My ten-year-old self had a word for this: poseur.

In reality, my whole career—my whole life, really—was a fraud. I was insecure, lonely, sad, and running from the Lord. If I were honest, I didn't even like scotch at the time, but it added to the persona I had created—and it helped me pass out at night to avoid my wife when I was in the States. When I was a latchkey kid at the age of six, I had to create a false self to protect my thoughts at night: *That wasn't a noise. That can't hurt me.* Now, the same protection mechanism was a weight around my neck, and not only could I no longer fight it, but I also didn't want to even try to break free anywhere because I was so tired of it all. *That wasn't a criticism. They can't hurt me.*

Those talks that I would give seemed interesting to people in the crowd and amazing to others who heard about it, but inside I was screaming for something real because those talks weren't. The substance may have been but not the sentiment. I felt the same in tenth grade when we read *Silas Marner*. Well, I never read it, but I still stood to give my presentation to my English class. Mr. Claroni called me out on it in front of everyone. "Mr. Duford," he said, "you're all histrionics with no substance. But . . ." he continued, "it was compelling and entertaining, so you got an A-." I had learned how to ride the back of my persona with the ease of an Olympic equestrian, but really, I was an insecure asshole by any measure because I didn't want to be found out as a fraud. I should have trusted my results and not questioned myself, but I was so unhappy I conflated the two. Unhappiness, it seemed, oozed from my pores, and because my histrionics were running thin—I didn't have the energy anymore—I could no longer cover it up.

That mask I wore was covering more than just a little boy without a father or a scared child at home alone but a man who was now scared to be known by anyone for fear of being hurt. You didn't like me? Well, that was the mask you didn't like, not me, so you couldn't hurt me. If you *did* like me? Well, that was the mask, too, so I didn't have to be vulnerable. That mask started to feel real, and that became a scary prospect to potentially face. Some days after transatlantic flights, I was so tired I couldn't decipher the difference between who I truly was and who I was pretending to be. The mask had started to graph to my skin.

It all came to a head for me at a talk in Boston after back-to-back flights had my brain so mushed up I didn't know where I was. My confidence and demeanor there in Beantown must've been sickening to others because I was unraveling from the inside out and started grasping for anything I could. I demanded an IPA to have on stage from the organizers because, if my illusion was slipping, I could buy an add-on prop to give my persona some more legs. When they declined, I said, "I don't care what your rules are; I'm not going on without one." They were so taken aback that they agreed. What a dick.

My talk was at 10:30 a.m., a bit too early to drink, but having that IPA—they found one from the closed hotel bar—drew a laugh from the crowd when, after I swilled some and put it down, I had said to everyone, "Oh you want one, too? Sorry, this is mine."

I only wore black on stage, which had become my signature look: a black T-shirt, black jeans, and my black Dr. Martens 1460s. I wouldn't realize the Johnny Cash similarity until years later. I had people laughing, learning, and wanting to learn more about digital marketing, which was silly, really, in the scheme of things, because while the substance was real, the delivery was on par with my tenth grade English project: all histrionics. *Is this my value? To feel wanted by a bunch of strangers because of my appearance and delivery?* I felt like I needed help, therapy, or something else to help me cope that didn't start with the word Glen.

My façade was starting to fall apart, with the life inside of me dying to break free, but the mask's hard shell kept it at bay. It was as if I lived in two realities, and after traveling between them so often, I had confused my own brain. Who did I want to be, really? I spent a lifetime wanting to be anyone else, never understanding how to just love myself enough to be me, scared no one would actually want that guy.

I wasn't that guy, yet I got caught up in all that persona's antics, thinking I could do whatever I wanted, whenever I wanted. Later, my therapist would tell me I probably acted out so much so that I would get caught and have my life change, which was probably true. I was reckless at my job, being riskier with projects, budget, and hiring than ever before. That in and of itself changed my track record from the exemplary executive the board of directors loved, to the one who had to be reined-in and kept at bay from derailing the business. I flew more, not just to get away, but to flaunt my travel on Instagram and to go on more trips than necessary: Hong Kong, Paris, Amsterdam, Tokyo, and more trips to London and New York. My travel budget was already twice my salary, but it even bloated from there. I was on a tear and did anything to avoid facing the conflict raging within.

Then, as if I felt my Teflon skin had no expiration date, I started ignoring my wife's needs, staying out late—when I was home in the States—and lying to her. I chatted with girls on Instagram, hit on my wife's friends, and flirted with other women at the office. I knew it wasn't who I was or wanted to be, but for a hot minute, it felt good to be wanted.

The holidays that year were rough. Between Thanksgiving—when I told my wife I was unhappy—and Christmas, I moved into the guest room and literally cried myself to sleep each night but would wake up in a cold sweat and stay awake for hours, trying to sort out where all of this had gone wrong. Who did I want to be? I felt like I was trapped in a Talking Heads' song: "How Did I Get Here?" When I finally would fall back to sleep, I wouldn't wake in time for my 5 a.m. call with London. I stopped working out. I kept drinking and moved on to Lagavulin Scotch at $99 a bottle, which would last only two days. *If I'm going to drink, I'll do it in style*, I thought.

About a week before Christmas, I had pulled into my garage and left my Jeep running while I closed the garage door behind me. I figured it was a painless way to escape this unhappiness. I'd fall asleep, and that would be the end of it. I then imagined my wife at the time and children coming home, driving into the spot next to me, together finding me, and I thought better of it. I opened the garage doors, turned off my Jeep, walked out of the driver's side through what was starting to be a thick fog of smoke, and breathed a new breath of fresh air outside.

On Christmas Eve, after the kids and my wife went to bed in their respective bedrooms, I retired to the guest room to watch a Netflix comedy show. That was when my iPhone notified me of a Facebook message.

"Hi, Kyle. We just now opened one present as we usually do on Christmas Eve, and when I opened one, it was from my good friend: a devotional for women," it started. "The page I opened to was Zephaniah 3:17, and the Lord immediately put you on my heart. I am praying he is healing you and loving you as he always has and will. Merry Christmas."

It was from Heather, my old friend from St. Louis, who I had dismissed twelve years earlier when I had walked away from my faith and everything—and everyone—who resembled a believer. She was the one who had mailed me a letter in 1997 with the same verse written in the letter, which pulled me out of my lowest point of depression in life until now. She still lived within a mile of her childhood home, but was now married with eight children, half adopted and half her own, with her husband, Micah.

Zephaniah 3:17, I thought. I looked up the verse online with my iPhone. I read it again and again, just like in '97. Tears welled in my eyes to the point I couldn't see. I had somehow forgotten the verse that I had tattooed on my left calf all those years ago. I lay there and thought: *Is there really a God out there? Did he still love me like he always claimed? Would he still quiet me with his love and hold me in his arms like Zephaniah promises us he will?*

I found it doubtful that this God of the Old Testament would care at all about a man who had run from him, forsaken him, denied him, and continued his fall into more sin without regard to anything.

I found it most doubtful indeed.

Within the first week of the new year, I had lost my job—how I lasted as long as I did with my spending and recklessness was a feat in and of itself—separated formally from my wife, and moved into a new, empty apartment. I was forty-two and life was pretty rough. I had been unhappy for nearly two decades, and this seemed inevitable to happen, I thought.

I reflected on that low moment in the garage, although now I wasn't doing much better. My new cement-floored apartment only had a bed on the floor, a TV, and a bike. I was lonely, sad, and ashamed. I was no longer with my wife because I had been reckless and selfish. I was reckless because I wasn't happy, and I wasn't happy because years earlier, I had walked away from Jesus.

Even through all of that, I felt God chasing me—though I couldn't explain how he was doing that apart from that weird Zephaniah note I had received. It was an odd feeling of being watched, as if everything I was doing in front of him was on full display, all my sin laid out before him. I felt exposed, vulnerable, and so full of shame. It had been more than twenty years since I had told Jesus I accepted him into my heart, and I was oblivious to the slow decline in my life ever since.

Without a job, my days were full of waking up, having coffee, going for a long bike ride, then watching Netflix the rest of the day. My severance and cashed-in vacation would hold me for a while, so I just did what I wanted. I just wasn't sure I wanted anything at all.

I lived on the sixth floor of a new high-rise apartment building and had a tiny balcony overlooking Ninth Avenue, exactly two hundred feet the way the crow flies from my former employer. I was afraid to open that balcony door because I wasn't sure if—on any particularly bad day—I'd crawl over the edge. I avoided that balcony at all costs.

Something had to change. That life wasn't working.

I had a bunch of airline miles and nothing but time to think, so I decided to go to Hawaii with my bicycle in a last attempt to return to the freedom and happiness I had once felt. If nothing else, I thought, it would be sunny and not cloudy, drizzly Portland weather.

Packing my shame with my bags, I left for the islands from the rain-soaked streets of the Pacific Northwest with my Canyon road bike stuffed into a bicycle box, a small duffle bag, and a copy of Brené Brown's *Daring Greatly* tucked under my arm.

While on board a little Alaskan Airline plane bound for Maui, I felt that I was supposed to learn something on that trip. I had this realization that I had lived a life of being closed-minded and withdrawn, giving no care to others. So, in a moment of reflection, I decided to say "yes" to anything that came my way on this trip (Similar to Jim Carrey's decision in *Yes Man*, though not as crazy). I'm not entirely sure what possessed me to make this deal with myself, but there I was, doing it. Telling God, or the universe—or whatever was out there—that I'd be open to whatever came my way once I landed in Kahului.

Jesus was listening.

Every day I ran, cycled, and took in new experiences.

"Oh, you're traveling alone? Do you want to join locals for a dinner party?" said a bartender.

"Yes," I said.

Then, the seventy-year-old Uber driver asked bluntly, "Do you want to sit up front?"

"Yes, of course," was my answer.

The stranger who saw me on my bike then asked, "Do you

want company tomorrow?"

"I'd love that! Yes," I said.

As I sat at a bar for a late lunch, I got the fresh tuna melt. A loud woman from New Jersey sitting to my left said, while staring at my sandwich, "Wow, that looks amazing! Can I have a bite?"

Now you should know this would normally never fly with me. I'd have not only discounted her but probably also made her feel awful for asking a stranger to eat his food. Then, perhaps, I'd ask to be reseated, loudly enough for her to hear me and feel awful. But that day, I said, "Sure," and happily gave her a bite. Then we chatted with my tuna fish and cheese hanging from the sides of her mouth. She had gone to my original college, Kutztown University, and she was in Maui, visiting her younger brother, Henry—seated to her left— who happened to ride bikes, too. She suggested he and I should ride together, and again, while I would've scoffed at this suggestion in the past, thinking it'd be a waste of time to ride with an older, slower man, we ended up riding together—twice. Both times he gave me a run for my money. Henry and I remain friends today.

Invariably, all of those people brought up Jesus in our conversation somehow, and at some point, they told me they believed he was their savior.

Those people and situations I would have dismissed easily just a week earlier with a scoff and snarky remark like I almost did to the older New Jersey lady from the bar, still munching on my sandwich with delight. I was protecting myself in the past, but by saying, "Yes," I experienced new interactions and experiences, and for the first time in a while, I started to let Jesus speak to my heart.

God met me in those interactions as I let people into my soul, my spirit. The list could go on: the tow-truck driver who came for my broken-down Jeep rental; the stranger who commented on my reading Brené Brown books in public; the sushi chef who asked about my meal; or the folks at the top of the Waihee Ridge Trail—all wonderful, Jesus-loving people. I had begun to see the light God had started to shine inside of me and *could actually be seen by others* if I opened up myself to them as the real me, an authentic me. This was a new, strange land I was wandering in, but it felt more like my skin than the mask's.

Even the couple from whom I rented an Airbnb room was part of his plan. The wife would have fresh-cut pineapple and Kona coffee waiting for me each morning when I woke up. The husband would ask me deep questions about tennis and computers (as deep as tennis and computer questions could be). They worried about me when the Jeep broke down and I came home late. They wished me luck and checked in on me as I left early one morning to climb Haleakala on my bicycle.

It was about the third morning when she asked, "Are you okay?"

"Of course," I said. "I'm fine. Thanks for the coffee!"

"No, I mean . . . are *you* okay, Kyle?" she asked like she was my grandmother.

I just looked down into my mug and started bawling. "No, no, I'm not." I shook my head.

"That's okay. I thought something was going on in your spirit. I could tell. We're Christians, and we just want you to know that we've been praying for you since you arrived."

They gave me a book on the Holy Spirit. They prayed for me, and I could hear them bless my bedroom for angels to be over me after I closed the door.

All those people were Christians. God was on the prowl. But would I listen? My "Yes Man" plan was for me to experience life; I didn't anticipate experiencing God. Even then, I probably needed to be convinced he still wanted me and loved me. And that he indeed was the one chasing me.

He saved his biggest surprise for last.

24 | CNN

*"I had human parents...they threw me into the ocean like I was
nothing. Somehow, I was rescued by the gods."*
— Maui, Disney's *Moana*

On my last day in Maui, I was sitting in Paia, a small surfing town
on the north shore. The legendary pipeline of left-hand breaks
crashing onto the shoreline drew surfers from around the world. It
was pretty much only visiting, or local—*kama'aina*—surfers here. You
could tell the locals by the uninterrupted tans on their feet. If there
were visible sandal lines on the tops of them, showing their white,
mid-western pale skin, they weren't locals. They were *haole*, not from
around here. I was haole, and I had the sandal lines to prove it.

In Paia, there's only one stoplight in town, at a three-way
intersection that merely acts to slow down the traffic from the main
road. The stem of the T that meets at that light runs right up to the
mountain town of Makawao—on the way up to Haleakala, the island's
dormant volcano and centerpiece. Her impressively deep crater is
home to the demigod Māui, who, according to legend, captured the
sun to force it to slow itself from setting, thus lengthening the day.

Go one way, and you'll soon be on the "Road to Hana," a vomit-inducing twenty-six-mile drive that winds through bamboo and eucalyptus forests, banana bread huts, and waterfalls. The locals won't head up there, so most of the cars coming down the mountain are heading to the airport town of Kahului.

Risk-takers come here for hikes, road bicycle ascents, or mountain bike descents. There's adventure to be had here in all directions with the longer Paian days, but here—at the intersection in the middle—is rest.

My rest—or adventure, depending on how you look at it—in Maui had lasted just over two weeks and included biking up the side of that very volcano—a daunting half-day excursion surprisingly with my old friend and coach, Chris Carmichael, who was coincidently guiding a ride up the same route—riding around the island's west side, and biking—not driving like the tourists—from Hana back down to Paia after a small commuter flight had taken my bike and me up the mountain earlier that morning.

I was exhausted and fulfilled, had ridden over three hundred miles in two weeks, laced up my running shoes for multiple runs and countless hikes, and drank probably a few hundred gallons of coffee and my share of IPAs. But the real deal was all the time in between, as I met countless bartenders, cyclists, store staff, Über drivers, tourists, locals, mailmen, concierges, and many others through my "yes" policy. It was different; it was enlightening. It was . . . good.

I had been consumed for years by greed, selfishness, and money. With a failed marriage in my rearview mirror and a loss of my three-year executive-level job, I needed to reconnect, to listen. To feel something. I was mostly dead inside, and the parts that were living weren't the ones of which I was proud: I had been afraid my whole life to be real and my authentic self. Who I was—who I *am*—inside is who I wanted the world to see. I wanted them to see the kind, gentle "teddy bear," as my daughter says, the guy who cries at *Mama Mia II* and other romantic plot lines, the guy who wasn't afraid to be me.

That was the man Jesus wanted twenty years ago under that Floridian tree. That was the guy he was chasing this whole time. I never knew that I could be allowed to be seen in public. I was so afraid to be rejected and unloved for being real that I spent my whole life wearing a mask.

In Maui, my goal was just to be open and unafraid, a task I was previously never able to grasp in life—for a day or an hour. It happened for two weeks, and it felt good. However, I could feel this tug in my spirit, and I knew there was something else.

Now here in Paia, I didn't want to leave. "Island life" did seem like a dream, and most tourists who came and visited didn't want to leave, either. Maybe it was because problems on the mainland seemed to stay there. Maybe it was the feeling of slightly longer days with more light—thanks to the lore of Maui's lassoing of the sun. For me, it was just new and safe, a place to be who I thought I always could have been. I just feared going back to . . . nothing—or worse—my old self.

My last meal on the island was in Paia—a very hoppy IPA and a small margarita pizza. I was sitting at Rock and Brews' sixteen-foot-long bar at the side of their restaurant full of picnic tables. Known for their pizzas and local fare—not to mention locals themselves, after long shifts on a boat or at a shop—it's a popular joint in this sleepy part of town. I decided to sit at the bar and relax before my overnight flight back to Portland, where absolutely nothing was waiting for me but an empty sixth-floor studio apartment.

I walked by the walls of the pub that were adorned with rock memorabilia and concert posters and headed to the restroom. There was a Woodstock replica poster from 1969. AC/DC. Kiss. Black Sabbath. An Elvis poster seemed out of place. Johnny Cash was prominent. The men's room was reserved for punk rock: The Clash hung above my urinal.

When I returned to my half-drank beer, I sank onto my bar stool and stared at the bank of television sets in front of me. Mostly all NFL Playoffs, mid-game. Since the Broncos were eliminated a few weeks earlier, I had no interest. So while I was waiting for my pizza, I decided to check the news on my *USA Today* app.

A headline on a video article read, "Evangelical: Don't Need a Christian President," and the title seemed interesting. It was the days and weeks following the Stormy Daniels/Donald Trump news, and I felt like this could be a good commentary on the situation—and even though I wasn't interested in the Christian part, as I look back, that was definitely a tug of the Holy Spirit in my heart.

I hit play on the video and had to wait the compulsory ten seconds for some sort of ad. I set my iPhone horizontally against the salt and pepper shakers, grabbed my IPA to take a swig, and glanced up at the ESPN television.

The pre-roll advertisement ended before I heard the most beautiful lisp in the world that I'd recognize anywhere, loud background noise or not:

> "I think they are focusing on the language and making excuses for it. Well, I don't really know that that was anybody's issue to begin with. I think it was, you know, the disheartening dehumanizing comments that were said around the world. I also think that—I said the last time I was on your program, Jim—my president doesn't have to be a Christian, but I don't want him to be held up as the poster boy for Christian evangelicals because he doesn't represent most of us."

Anchor Jim Sciutto asked another question, but I was mesmerized. I was looking at my Jerushah on television—my Jerushah!

I hadn't seen or talked to her in twenty-one years! Now she was speaking her heart and blowing me away with her words. She was wearing a blue dress, her hair was a bit longer and wavier than it was once curly, and she looked gorgeous. There was that little birthmark, her mannerisms. She was my "What if?" person. I was rapt and kept watching her and listening to her bold words.

> "I understand a lot of evangelicals are supporting him because of his policies. I'd love to see a Christian leader come out and say that they support Trump for his policies but that his behavior disgusts them and he needs to clean up his act."

I had thought about this countless times in the last two decades, in countless ways, how I would see her again. *Would I run into her on the streets of Manhattan? Would I find her waiting for me outside a book signing (though admittedly, I'd have had to have written a book first)? Maybe she just called a friend of a friend of a friend—though we had no common friends—and started talking?* Dreams, all of them.

I never knew her married name, and I couldn't find her in the early days of the internet. When Facebook finally was released to non-students, she was the first one I looked up. Having a name like hers, she wasn't difficult to find—although you'd be surprised how many Jerushahs there are. When I did find her, I couldn't bring myself to write to her. She had a husband and children. She must've been so happy.

I immediately looked her up on Facebook again, and this time fired off a note through Messenger. I didn't know why I felt the need to write to her, but I did. It was brief but poignant: "Hi, Jerushah, I'm not sure if you remember me, but I just saw you on TV, and . . . well, I just wanted to let you know that what you did in one and half minutes did more for women, minorities, Christians, and immigrants than I've seen in the last two years. Hope you're well, Kyle."

Now my heart was thumping. I could barely finish my beer. I went back and watched her interview again and again, and then a notification came over my screen, a reply.

"Kyle Duford. Of course, I remember you. We were engaged! Thank you for the kind note. I hate doing these interviews, but I end up doing them anyway. I hope you're well."

We exchanged a few more lines of niceties but called it a day. She was on East Coast time, and it was getting pretty late, she said. I said it was lovely speaking and said goodbye.

What was Jesus doing in my life? Was this confirmation—after all these Christians in Maui showing up for me—that he was saying, "Hey, remember me?"

I knew one thing, though, that if I were God, and I wanted Kyle to know I was real, I would bring her back into his life. I had no idea what he was planning.

I couldn't think about anything else on that flight home to Portland. A wave of *something* washed over me, and it was the first time I had felt calm in a very long time. My anxiety about life seemed to vanish on that flight. I was still lost, but at least I had the map to help me find my way.

Was this what it was like with Jesus in my life, for real? Is this what other people—"real" Christians—feel? That calm felt like I didn't need to worry about the future. Was this how others lived? I hadn't picked up a Bible or read scripture in nearly twenty years, but a verse I once had memorized in high school somehow popped into my head: "Therefore do not worry about tomorrow, for tomorrow will worry about itself." (Matt 6:34)

I slept soundly on the plane. I dreamed of Jerushah, and I woke up on the runway in Portland.

25 | REWRITE THE STARS

"How do we rewrite the stars?
Say you were made to be mine?
Nothing can keep us apart
'Cause you are the one I was meant to find"
—From *The Greatest Showman*

It was a sad, tragic day when a shooter came into Marjory Stoneman Douglas High School in Parkland, Florida, just outside Ft. Lauderdale, and killed seventeen people and wounded seventeen more. It was Valentine's Day in 2018, and I was shaken. With three children myself, I felt for those parents and wept for the students. I cried in my empty apartment and fell asleep with the news on the television.

When I woke on the morning of the 15th, the reporters were broadcasting outside the school. They showed a wide shot, and I thought I was seeing something from a dream. *Did I have the news on all night?* I must've recognized it from the previous reporting.

Then it hit me: it was Jerushah's high school. I texted her through Facebook again.

"I'm sorry to bother you again," I wrote. "But is that your old high school on the news?"

An hour later, she wrote back. "OMG, Kyle. How on earth do you remember that?"

"Well," I said. "Of course I remember. We were engaged." I used the line back on her, trying to be a little flirtatious.

"Fair, fair. Yes, it is really sad. My nephew was sending me videos from inside the school."

"Wow. That's crazy. Is he okay?"

"Yeah, everyone we know is fine. It's Aram's son, Riley. Remember Aram?"

I did, her brother. "Yeah, yeah, I remember Aram. How is he?"

We talked about her five brothers, most of whom I had met when we were engaged previously, but the two I knew best were Aram and Tullian, the two closest in age above her. We would hang out together back then, and I really enjoyed them as brothers and as friends. Both, I learned, were divorced, broken, and rebuilding their lives. Both involved infidelity. It gave me an off sense of comfort to feel like I wasn't alone in my brokenness.

We talked about the last two decades over text, as best you can over text, basically saying how we were doing and other niceties. Before it ended, I just casually said, "We should catch up sometime," and I typed in my number.

My phone rang immediately.

We did a lot of catching up on that phone call. We discussed why and when we had broken up—neither of us could remember. We talked about the fun we'd had in Boulder, Colorado. We reminisced about my asking her dad's permission to marry her. I told her about how I tried to find her through Johnny Cash so long ago, realizing she never would've known that or about the tattoo I had gotten in Hebrew of Zephaniah after I had lost her.

Although much had transpired since we last had seen each other, we felt safe talking about our lives together. She was safe because we had history, but we didn't know the same people. It wasn't as if we'd bumped into each other or each other's exes. There was something easy about talking to her, too. I didn't need to re-learn her at all, just catch up on her life. We clicked like we had in college. It was refreshing. She told me of her three children, one adopted, living in Greenville, South Carolina. She also wasn't happy, either. Turned out, she was seeking authenticity as well and was also reading Brené Brown's *Daring Greatly* for the same reason as me. We talked for a while about our faults, our issues, how fake we both felt. I told her about my divorce and my quest to be authentic. I told her about my therapy sessions and how I was trying to work through being a divorced man.

Jerushah took me as the broken man I was. I took her as the broken woman she was. We made a deal. "Since you're so far away," she said. "I feel safe telling you my truths. You know, being authentic—for once. It's not like you'd tell anyone my secrets. I feel like I can trust you."

"Yeah, of course, you can trust me. We were going to get married!" I said. "I would never violate your trust. Besides, I feel like I can trust you—you're a safe person for me, too."

"Well, let's have a deal. No matter what, we're always honest with each other."

"Oh yeah, of course," I said.

"No, like I mean, *always*. Even when it's hard."

"Got it," I said. "Honest always, even when hard."

"There," she said. "So now tell me the real bits about your life."

And that was just what I did. I told her about walking away from my faith shortly after we had broken up. I told her about my failed relationships, how I saw myself, and where I wrongly placed my value. I would lay each shameful item from the past out for her to see me in all my brokenness: my insecurities, my selfish ambition, my vanity, and the value I saw in climbing the corporate ladder. Each time she took it in, talked me through it, and there was never any judgment. The larger the transgression didn't matter. Things I wouldn't scream into a Coke bottle before throwing it into the ocean suddenly left my lips as if I were in confession. I explained how I was running ever since the last time she had seen me, that I was aimless in a world where I questioned Jesus, but I felt him chasing me. I told her about that time in the garage and then second-guessing it. No matter the story, she took me as I was, and through her, I started to see how Jesus saw me, too.

Our conversations continued on and off throughout the coming months. When she needed to talk about her separation, a problem with her kids, or just have a laugh, she'd call. I would call when I wanted to hear her voice, ask her something about scripture, or tell her about my therapy. I was living in a town where most of my friends were lost due to the divorce, so I was thankful to have such a dear friend, only a phone call away, to help me talk through and figure out my purpose and my future. She, also struggling with lost friendships because people assumed the worse of her divorce, confided her fears, thoughts, and hurt.

Then, one day a few months later, I was driving home in my Jeep Wrangler on Interstate 5 to Portland from southern Oregon, where I was riding my bike that day. Jerushah and I had just hung up after another four-hour phone call. I was falling in love again with the same woman but in a new, fresh way. I took a risk letting her in to know the real me, even though I was just learning who I was myself, but I feared my heart would break yet again if I fell for her.

I looked over at my phone resting on the passenger seat and started to cry as the rain began to fall. My windshield wipers were slapping back and forth as the marble-sized raindrops were slamming into the windshield. It seemed the more I cried, the more rain came down. I was questioning why God would bring her back into my life—and feared the same rejection and loss again. I was so confused. Cries turned to anger as I screamed at the Lord at the top of my lungs. "What do you fucking *want* from me? What do you want from me?" I screamed so loud my throat hurt: "Why me? Why now? Why are you chasing me? Why her? What . . . do . . . you . . . *want*?"

At that moment, right there in a pouring-down rainstorm, I clearly heard the Lord as if I heard someone talk into my ear. Not an audible voice, but his voice, a take-hold-of-you-and-look-you-in-the-eye type of voice, and it was unmistakable. "Stop denying me, and I got you." I *felt* those words as if they were clear as day.

I couldn't speak. I didn't know what to say. So I thought for what seemed like an eternity but was most likely a millisecond, then right then and there I said, "Okay, Lord. Okay. You win," and I recommitted my life to Jesus that day outside of Salem, Oregon.

I suddenly knew what he wanted from me. He wanted me all along. I felt like I had come home and found my father waiting there, arms outstretched with joy in anticipation.

Although I had forgotten about his love, he not only remembered me, but he never had forgotten me. I realized his grace had been shown to me by the many people throughout my life, even the strangers in Hawaii, and now the woman I had loved for twenty-one years. I finally understood what Paul meant in Ephesians. "Not by works, so that no one can boast" (Eph 2:9).

The rain immediately stopped. So did the agonizing pain. The old was gone. The new had come.

26 | STARTING OVER

"Oh, simple thing, where have you gone?
I'm getting old, and I need something to rely on
So, tell me when you're gonna let me in
I'm getting tired, and I need somewhere to begin."
—Keane, "Somewhere Only We Know"

I stopped denying God, and true to his form, it was the next day when I had a chance to show my mettle. "You're not a Christian, are you?" I was asked with a little sarcasm or disdain. That wasn't an uncommon question, or manner, in the Pacific Northwest—the world of timber, craft beer, and coffee—as it certainly was not the Bible belt. That geographical fact served all the more reason to be on my heels when I was asked that question, each day, every day, for about three weeks. "You're not a Christian, are you?" they'd say. It was the opposite of Maui. Instead of being told what someone else was about, I was being asked what I was about.

I stopped denying God, and true to his form, it was the next day when I had a chance to show my mettle. "You're not a Christian, are you?" I was asked with a little sarcasm or disdain. That wasn't an uncommon question, or manner, in the Pacific Northwest—the world of timber, craft beer, and coffee—as it certainly was not the Bible belt. That geographical fact served all the more reason to be on my heels when I was asked that question, each day, every day, for about three weeks. "You're not a Christian, are you?" they'd say. It was the opposite of Maui. Instead of being told what someone else was about, I was being asked what I was about.

"Yes, I am," I would say, and then continue, "I don't know what that means, and I'm probably bad at being one, but yes, I am a Christian." I would be lying if I told you I wasn't nervous; I probably could have turned coal into diamonds by the strength of my tightly clenched hands, but I had made a deal with God, and I was going to live up to my end.

In those three weeks or so, I would call Jerushah and tell her all the stories. "This just happened, the barista at Stumptown Coffee asked me, 'You're not a Christian, are you?'" I told her. Jerushah wasn't surprised; she knew first-hand how God had moved in my life. "Can I guess what you said?" she would ask, chuckling, knowing full well that I would say "Yes" each time.

As I was learning to balance while standing on my new Christian legs, Jerushah started showing me glimpses into her life. She introduced me to pop culture, which I always thought was silly for adults to enjoy. In reality, however, I was both too full of myself and scared to let my hair down to enjoy these simple pleasures. Many of her favorite musicians I had heard of but skipped over them with the notion that they were too poppy or trivial, such as Justin Bieber, Taylor Swift, Demi Levato, and Mumford & Sons. She made me playlists with these and other artists like Avett Brothers, Camila Cabello, Ben Rector, and Rachel Platten—none of which I had heard of. She sent a song by Platten called "Better Place," and I wept as I read the lyrics:

But it feels like I've opened my eyes again

And the colors are golden and bright again
There's a song in my heart, I feel like I belong
It's a better place since you came along

That was me. Everything seemed to be brighter from my previous black and white—and mostly gray—life since I had found love again. Those experiences, those minutes and hours of life, provided little cherries on top of my days. Like the movie *Pleasantville*, it felt all of sudden as if everything was now in technicolor.

I hadn't eaten in a fast-food restaurant in twenty years, often scoffing at those who did. "You've never had Chick-fil-A nuggets?" Jerushah asked surprisingly. "What did you feed your kids on road trips? Did you pack bento boxes?" We laughed, largely because that was just what I had done.

I devoured those chicken nuggets—and fries—and realized simple pleasures are amazing—especially in moderation. I also started drinking Diet Coke by the gallon, loving its taste, fizzes, and lack of calories. I was living my best life—damn the onlookers. Jerushah had opened my eyes to a life full of joy and happiness, the complete opposite of the life I had been living.

But she also had changed. "It's refreshing to have you as my activity," she told me over text in anticipation of our next rendezvous. "To just . . . be together. Not needing my phone when I'm with you or wishing I was somewhere else. I don't want to be anywhere else—you're my home."

I wanted to tell her I loved her. But I was nervous. *Is this stupid? Will she reciprocate?*

"Hey, can I tell you something?" I texted.

"Of course," she said.

"I'm calling you."

"Okay," she answered via text mere seconds before I rang.

"I just wanted to say . . . you know . . . just that . . ."

"Yeah?" she asked.

"Um, well. I just . . . wanted to say that . . ."

"Kyle, what is it?" she asked.

"Oh, fuck it. I love you."

"I know you do, Kyle. And I adore you," she said. "But I want to wait until I see you in person before I tell you."

"You didn't need to say anything. I just wanted you to know."

"You know how I feel about you. I just want to tell you in person. But if we ever get married, that should be in our vows," she laughed.

"What part?"

"The 'eff-it' part, dork."

"Deal."

It was shortly after that conversation that we traveled to see each other a few times, discovering how much we enjoyed traveling together, exploring life together, and even our quiet moments. We had years to catch up on, and we did just that, over the phone, text, and these short trips in which we were able to meet up. During one of those quick trips over a long weekend, she looked at me over coffee and said simply, "I want to be your wife." Then we both smiled. *I've been waiting for this almost my entire life,* I thought.

"Well, I *want* you to be my wife. Let's make that happen." I said, "I think I should move to Greenville."

She smiled and kissed me. We both took mental pictures of the moment.

"I can come this next weekend and look for places to live."

"Yeah?" she said. "Okay, let's do this."

"Wait!" I said suddenly. "I'm supposed to go to Hawaii this weekend and train with Henry for the Race to the Summit Ride."

(Henry and I had remained friends since meeting his older sister over my accidentally shared tuna fish sandwich in Maui.)

I could hear the disappointment in her voice when she merely said, "Oh."

"You know what?" I asked. "I'm calling Delta now. It was on miles anyway; I'll switch the trip to Greenville. I'll come look at places instead."

"You will?"

"I will," I said.

She smiled. If we were going to be partners, I was going to sacrifice my fair share and show her how much I loved her. *She wants to be my wife!* was all I was thinking.

We took off for home later that day from the same terminal, our gates across from each other, so we stayed together as long as we could before we hugged goodbye and said, "I'll see you this weekend." She turned around to Gate 34, me to 35.

After boarding and finding my aisle seat, I popped in my AirPods and turned on a cycling podcast from Lance Armstrong, whose voice came booming into my world:

"Hey, everybody, and welcome to The Forward Podcast. Before we start, let me tell you we're broadcasting live this week from George Hincapie's Hotel Domestique in Greenville, South Carolina. Now, listen, guys, if you're a cyclist at all, and you haven't been *here*—you need to come to Greenville. It's epic riding. Okay, let's get started with the show . . ."

I don't typically believe in signs, but this was one I refused to ignore. I was going to move to Greenville.

That week back in Portland, I was presenting a proposal to an old friend of mine who needed just six weeks of marketing help at his company. It was a perfect amount of time to close up my apartment, get ready, and move across the country. My ex-wife was moving out of state in a similar time frame, so everything was lining up. I just needed this quick consulting gig to be able to pay for it all.

As I walked into his office, a glass-walled square in the center of his floor, flanked on all sides by cubicles, I was giddy. Things were finally falling into place. All I had to do was trust in Jesus, whose words echoed in my head: "Stop denying me, and I got you."

My friend, George, welcomed me and offered me a seat on his sofa. Before I could even get out my proposal, he said, "I hear you're moving to South Carolina!?" (Our kids went to the same school, and parents must've talked, as parents do at kids' schools). "Why would ya want to move there?" he asked condescendingly. "A bunch of redneck, hillbilly, conservative, born-again Republicans in a state with one of the worst education systems in the country? What are you, a Christian or something?"

I was stunned. In a millisecond, my mind flashed through the consequences of my possible answers: If I were to say yes, I could lose nearly a $20,000 assignment. Say no, and . . . well, you know by now I wasn't going to say no.

"Yeah," I blurted. "Yeah, I am. And I'm learning how to be a Christian again. But yes." I had surprised myself how easily that had come out.

"Oh. Okay," he said.

"Anyway, listen," I said. "I have a great proposal here for you, and I think you're going to love my ideas for this campaign."

The next forty-five minutes were easy. It was fun, and I was able to relax again. George and I laughed and talked after we went through the proposal. He was engaged in our conversation and leaning on every word.

I got the contract.

Six weeks later, I packed up my things from the office and presented my final recommendations. Then I went home, packed, hitched a U-Haul to my Jeep, and loaded them both up with everything I owned, which admittedly, wasn't much.

My brother, Christian, offered to help me move down to South Carolina, but he couldn't take Thursday off work, the day I needed to leave, if I wanted to make it down in time for the Fourth of July.

"If you can make it to Salt Lake City," he offered. "I'll fly in there and finish the drive with you."

I agreed.

The last time we had driven that far together—or even spent this much time together—was in 1994 when we drove from Minneapolis to Philadelphia, mostly in a snowstorm, eating only McDonald's along the way—the most recent time I remember having had any fast food.

This trip would be different.

My friend, Pér, came over Wednesday night to help me pack the U-Haul. Packing was a challenge. It wasn't the amount but the awkwardness of the stuff, and the tiny elevator meant many trips, but we were able to get it all loaded within two hours, locked up, and ready to go.

In the morning, I drove the Jeep over to my children's school and said goodbye. They were leaving for Denver the next morning and were equally excited. I would fly to see them there in a month, but that goodbye was particularly painful. We would no longer be a few minutes apart. But I didn't second guess my decision to move to Greenville. I knew I couldn't be who I knew needed to be if I stayed in Portland or moved to Denver—I feared I would backslide. I think they had started to see a change in me and perhaps welcomed a new life for us all. I'd like to think so, anyway.

The drive to Salt Lake was nearly eight hundred miles and fourteen hours, longer than it would've been without towing a trailer. I passed the time with some podcasts, phone calls, and more Diet Cokes than you could imagine was possible to consume. I made it to the airport just in time to snag my brother, hit a local hotel, and crash for night one. We were both so tired, we just fell asleep.

We rose in the morning on a gorgeous day to drive—sunny, bright-blue skies, and near 80°F. We grabbed some buffet eggs and set across the Rockies on Interstate 80, driving through Wyoming and the bulk of Nebraska before stopping in Lincoln, just outside of Omaha. (A former Colorado Buffalo willingly stopping in the land of the Nebraska Cornhuskers meant we were tired; I ignored the old archaic collegiate faux pas.) In a drive-thru in Cheyenne, Wyoming, my FaceTime rang from Jerushah. She and her youngest, Ali, were on the other side. It was Ali's tenth birthday and my first time meeting her.

"*Hi,*" she said excitedly.

"Hi there," I said. "Happy birthday!"

"Thank you. We're having Chick-fil-A for birthday lunch!"

"You know what's crazy? I just had Chick-fil-A for the *first time* ever the other day with your mom."

She looked at her mom as if to say, "Is he being serious?" she nodded.

"Wow," she said. "I love Chick-fil-A."

"Me, too!"

Ali was adopted by Jerushah and her ex-husband and is explosive with emotion in all directions. When she's happy—she's *really happy,* and when she's mad, she's *really mad.* I love this about her. What you see is what you get. She's half white and half African American, and her resulting complexion is stunning. If you know the young actress Zendaya, Ali's doppelganger, then you have a good idea of how many boys I'll have to scare off in a few years.

We each had to pay for our own food, so we said our good-byes and I told her I couldn't wait to meet her in person. She still boasts to people that she was the first of her siblings to meet me.

"*Bye!*" said Ali, "I can't wait to see you in a few days!"

Day three was another fourteen hours into Nashville—so close to my new home that I couldn't handle it, but I couldn't get into my apartment until the next day anyway, so no reason to push ourselves. I was so giddy and nervous; we were so close. Christian and I slept well, and the next day we were in Greenville in time for lunch.

We rolled into town on July 3, pulling into my complex the same moment that Jerushah did with some drinks and food for us. Ali was with her. We all said hello to each other. I introduced my brother, and then we started unpacking in a fury. Earlier that weekend, a new sofa sleeper was delivered, timed to ensure my brother had a place to sleep. My apartment was small but perfect. A one-bedroom flat on the ground floor, one block from Jerushah's place in one direction and one block from the twenty-mile Swamp Rabbit Trail in the other.

I was in my new town in my own little place, ready to start my life over with meaning, purpose, and authenticity.

But first, I had to meet the other two children.

27 | THE CHILDREN
"Beauty begins the moment you decide to be yourself."
—Coco Chanel

The first chance we had, Jerushah and I made arrangements to have dinner with Anabelle, her eldest daughter, who had just turned seventeen. It was less than a week since I had moved to town, and we were dying to meet each other. The plan was to meet her for dinner, and then her boyfriend would join afterward to play some air hockey and arcade games together.

Anabelle was already at the restaurant in downtown Green-ville when Jerushah and I approached, holding hands. "She's never seen me with anyone other than her father," Jerushah explained as we arrived. "And we never held hands."

Great, make me more nervous as we walk in.

Once inside, we saw Anabelle sitting at a table. I introduced myself to Anabelle and sat down. Jerushah sat down across from her daughter to my left; we held hands tightly. As I looked at Anabelle, I noticed a big tear had welled up in her right eye, and it dripped onto her cheek.

"Sweetie, what's wrong?" said Jerushah.

"I've just . . . I've just . . ." she stuttered.

"Belle, what is it?" her mom repeated. "Was this too soon? This was too soon."

"No, Mom, that's not it at all," she said. "I've just never seen you . . . happy. You're smiling, Mom!"

Jerushah started tearing up, too, and I was one step ahead of her as usual.

"Well, that's why I wanted you to meet him. This is what Kyle has done for me. I'm able to be me again, honey. *This* is who I am."

Anabelle looked at us lovingly. She was taking a mental photo.

"I loved him before, Belle, and I love him now," Jerushah said. "He's my person."

Anabelle looked at me. "Thank you for loving my mom," she said. "I've heard so much about you, and I have so many questions for you."

"I'm not going anywhere," I said. "Ask away."

"You better not go anywhere," said Anabelle. "It seems I just got my best friend back."

We spent the night over dinner talking about Anabelle, her ambitions, her schooling, and her new boyfriend, who I was about to meet. She reminded me of her mom at the same age when we had first met: ambitious, confident, and beautiful.

The evening with Anabelle and her boyfriend flew by. When we said goodbye later on in the evening to the kids, Anabelle gave me a big-squeeze hug, and I kissed her on the cheek. "I really was looking forward to meeting you, Anabelle," I said. "I look forward to getting to know you better."

"Me, too—Dad!" she said. Then she laughed hysterically. "I'm just kidding!" she yelled as she walked away. "Love you, Mom."

The next night it was Liam's turn, a completely different type of kid. "Just be yourself," said Jerushah. "Be authentic."

Liam was fifteen, loved Rubik's Cubes and games, probably on the autism scale somewhere, and had a rating system for how good tortilla chips were, ranking them in order of thickness.

"The thinnest ones are the best," he explained. "These are about a four on the scale of ten," he said as he plunged said chip into the queso and then shoved it into his mouth.

Jerushah had told me that when she had first told Liam about me, he was a bit indifferent. That was, until she told him I couldn't wait to meet him because I thought he was cool. That was true. I couldn't wait to meet this kid, and from the stories I had heard, he seemed like an older version of my son, Jackson.

"He wants to meet *me*?" he apparently asked.

"Yeah," said his mom. "He really does."

"Does he like Mexican?" asked Liam. "Because if so, let's do it."

Tonight was the Mexican night, and while there were no tears like Anabelle or enthusiasm like Ali-bug, Liam was all about questions.

"Where are you from?"

"What do you do?"

"I heard you contracted with Nike. Is that true?"

And of course, the obligatory "What are your intentions with my mother?"

Those weren't asked throughout the night but rather in machine-gun rapid-fire, so I answered them as quickly as I could in return.

"Uh, let me see," I said. "Portland. Executive. Yes. And I want to marry her one day."

"Okay, okay, okay," said Liam, nodding with each word. He then took a chip and held it up, focusing on it. "Yeah, this may be actually a three on the chip scale."

"See, I like thick chips," I said. "So, on your scale, maybe a seven to an eight?"

"So . . . thick chips, eh?" he asked.

"I think so," I said. "But I've only been here to this place. Maybe you and I can try some other places you like, and you can show me the best thin chips in town?"

Jerushah was just watching all this to see if she needed to offer me any air cover.

"Just . . . you and me?" said Liam.

"Heck, yeah," I said. "Just two guys on the town, scoping out the best chips. Sounds like a blast."

He looked at his mom. "Can I go do that?"

"Of course, Lele," she said, calling him by his nickname— which I would later find out was short for Lele the Dinosaur.

"Really?" he said, then turned to me. "Mom says I can go!"

"Great!" I said as if I hadn't heard her.

Jerushah gave me a wink that Liam couldn't see, which told me, "Good job," without words.

That was how I won Liam over—tortilla chips.

The three kids, Jeru, and I would often spend time together, but we intentionally tried to go at a slow pace; I eased myself into their lives. I didn't come over for dinner every night or try to meet them every time they went out to eat. The goal was to give them time to get used to us. That didn't last long. Pretty soon, they wanted me over every night.

As a divorced mother with kids' schools and activities in all directions, Jerushah welcomed my help, and I quickly assimilated to my new partner role; for example, while one of us took Ali down the road to elementary school, the other would take Liam to middle school. Then, we'd meet up afterward for a workout together.

Anabelle was another story. Already self-sufficient, she would wake up early and drive herself to school where she'd learn through midday, and then she'd drive to work at a family's house and nanny until well after six in the evening. Most of the time after her work, she'd spend time with her boyfriend.

All three kids would split their time between their father's house and Jerushah's. Sundays, Monday, and Tuesday nights were all at Jerushah's, whereas Wednesday, Thursday, and Fridays, they would be at the other home. We'd alternate weekends.

Anabelle struggled the most with this arrangement, bouncing back and forth, so when she turned eighteen in the middle of her senior year, she rented a small apartment about half a mile from her mother's apartment. To help her establish her credit and get her the apartment, I co-signed on anything she needed. I had earned her trust. And she didn't just trust me with her finances, but she also trusted me with her questions about life, love, her struggles with her father—which were eerily similar to mine as a child—and big decisions in life. She knew I would do anything for her. I stepped up to the role gladly, knowing that being fatherless didn't mean I couldn't step in and be a dad.

So there we were, this amalgam of a family, tied to each other through love, albeit informally. I had an apartment across the street where I'd sleep, but for all intents and purposes, we were a family. Ana was out most of the time, or at her own place, so it was usually the four of us—Jeru, Ali, Liam, and me—all throughout that winter hunkering down around a tiny little circular dining room table, eating tacos or chicken and rice.

My oldest child, Logan, was busy being a goalkeeper in college and hadn't yet made the trip to see us all, but when my younger two children flew in to visit for Thanksgiving and the two weeks following Christmas, we had a blast. They got along with each other so well, it was hard to tell which family was which as both sides happily, graciously, and lovingly accepted each other. Logan and Anabelle met up for coffee when they were in the same town—they were exactly six months apart—and talked about boys and college and life. It was quite the crew, but we weren't yet on the same ship. I looked forward to making this a real family.

28 | NEW YORK CITY

"Oh, Brooklyn, Brooklyn, take me in
Are you aware the shape I'm in?
My hands they shake, my head it spins
Oh, Brooklyn, Brooklyn, take me in"
—The Avett Brothers, "I and Love and You"

I planned to sit Jerushah's kids down at Starbucks in downtown Greenville, across from Falls Park, a block from her apartment. It was a cold, crisp night. I was meeting up with Anabelle, a spitting image of her mother at the same age, who had just turned eighteen. Liam, her only boy, was fifteen, and Ali, or "Ali-bug," our nickname for her firecracker of an adopted daughter, was only ten.

"What's up?" asked Ali-bug, sitting across from me at a small table, hot chocolate in hand. It was a cold night in February, and she was warming up.

"Well, guys," I said. "I want to talk to you about something very important."

"Oh my gosh, am I in trouble?" asked Liam.

"Ha, no, buddy. You're not in trouble."

"Are we getting a dog?" asked Anabelle, knowing full well we already had two in the house.

"No, kiddo. No more dogs," I said, chuckling.

"Then . . . what?" asked little Ali-bug.

"Well, guys, you know how much I love your mother and how much she means to me, right?"

"And us, too?" semi-questioned Ali-bug.

"Yes, yes, of course. I love you all very much."

"Oh," said Ali-bug in relief, "then what?"

"Well, I think you all know we'd like to get married."

"No kidding," said Liam. "You practically are now."

"Sure, sure, we spend all of our time together, yes. That's because we love each other very much."

"We know you're getting married one day, Kyle," said Anabelle, sitting to my right, scrolling through Instagram on her phone.

"I suppose you do."

"Can I go call my girlfriend?" asked Liam.

"In a minute. . . . I want to talk to you about this."

"Kyle, what is it?" asked Anabelle.

"I want to be sensitive to you three. This is a big decision."

They looked at each other, then at me, as if to say, "No kidding."

I pulled a ring box out of my pocket and held it up. "This is a big deal, guys. I need to ask you all something." I didn't open it.

"Okay," they all said in their own way. For Liam, that was merely a nod.

"I love your mother," I said as tears started welling up in my eyes. "And I want to ask her to marry me this weekend while we're in New York together."

New York was a special place for us. We both loved the city, and it was a dream for us both to live there at some point, maybe for a year, and just experience it. We typically went to New York every three months or so, and we had it down to a science: cheap flight from Greenville to Newark, NJ, where we grabbed a $14 train ticket to Penn Station in Midtown. We then walk to a nearby hotel which we only found after weeks of searching for the best deal—close to Midtown, with a fitness studio and at least one treadmill.

Half the time, we visit the same places: Eataly on 23rd, Fifth Avenue for shopping, China Town for dumplings, and Central Park for running. We visit Bryant Park in the winter for raclette cheese on baguettes for dinner, and in the summer, we visit the park to lounge on the grass, drinking vodka sodas. Everyone needs a certain person to experience NYC in the same way as yourself, and Jerushah and I fit each other's mold perfectly. We walk at the same pace, enjoy the same food, and want to do the same things—even if that means visiting multiple Madewell stores to ensure we find exactly the right size, usually an extra small, to purchase the perfect piece of apparel for her work.

New York City. It was the perfect place to propose.

"Is that the ring?" asked Anabelle. "Can I try it on?"

"No, Anabelle, you can't," I said as I turned to look at all the children. "Look, guys, I know your dad got engaged without talking to you first, and now he's getting married next weekend without you there. I want you to really think about this. Will it be weird if I ask her this weekend? Will you be upset at all? Because I don't want that—at all."

"Can I come to the wedding?" asked Ali-bug.

"Yes, of course, you can come to the wedding. Kids, can I have your permission to marry Mom?"

Anabelle started crying, which led me to cry. Ali-bug was sucking down her cocoa, perplexed at the emotion.

"You're already like a stepfather to us," said Anabelle, sniffling away tears. "I've never seen Mom so happy. You changed her life. Because of you, we have our mom back. She is the mom we always thought she could be."

"So . . ." I said while wiping my tears.

"Yes!" said Anabelle. "You can marry her!"

"Liam?" I looked at him questioningly.

"Yeah, for sure," he said. "I think of you as a dad already."

"But I can come, right?" persisted Ali-bug. "Can I be *in* it?"

"You guys can all be in it. We *want* you in it."

"Yay!" she said.

"Can I go now?" said Liam. "You know, call my girlfriend?"

"Can we see the ring?" said Anabelle.

I finally opened the box and showed them.

"Wow!" said Ali-bug.

"Is that *real*?" asked Liam. The kid had a question about everything.

"Yes, it's real," I said.

"How much is it worth?" he asked.

"Liam!" scolded Anabelle. "You can't ask that!" She looked at me. "You'll tell me later, right?"

I laughed. "Probably not, kiddo."

I had instantly fallen in love with these kids in the previous year and had been treating them as my own, so they, too, needed to be a part of the decision. I was altering their life, and they deserved a say. Soon, we would all be living under one roof, at least them with us fifty percent of the time, and I wanted their blessing, much like I had wanted Jerushah's dad's blessing over two decades before.

"Okay, guys. I love you. All of you." I scanned the table and looked them each in the eye. "I really do."

"We know," said Ana. "We love you, too."

"I love you, Kyle," said Liam.

"I love you, too!" said Ali-bug.

"It's not a contest, Ali," said Liam.

With that, we all dispersed. Anabelle went back to her apartment, just a mile from us, Liam walked back the long way so he could make his phone call, and Ali-bug grabbed my hand and we beelined it back to their apartment. As far as Jerushah knew, I had only taken her to get hot chocolate.

She squeezed my hand and looked up at me. "You love me, right?"

"I love you so much, Ali-bug."

"Good. You can marry my mom. For real." She smiled. "But I want to be there!"

We arrived at the Ace Hotel in Midtown and went straight to our room. We were tired from the flight, which had been delayed, and since we had awoken early for the drive to Charlotte to catch our flight, exhaustion had set in.

Jerushah needed to close her eyes, and I needed to get some work sorted out, so I went to the lobby to work. I snagged a local IPA from the bartender and hunkered down with my MacBook at the counter, but I couldn't think straight. I was distracted and nervous. I had no idea when I was going to pop the question or what I was going to say.

I opened my notebook to a blank page in the back and just started writing down my feelings, trying to find the right words or series of sentiments.

The first time I laid eyes on you—January or so of 1997—I was so taken by you. Your smile. Your eyes. Your body. After we first spoke, I knew there was so much to love. Your intelligence was evident right away.

What I cared about is that you loved Jesus. I tried to love him then, but you showed me how to be genuine—I just wouldn't understand that for another twenty-one years.

I started to tear up. I wrote and wrote and wrote until my hand hurt and two sides of a large Moleskine were filled with small handwriting and drops of tears. I told her everything I was feeling: how she had saved me, how in those interim twenty-one years I had messed up life badly, but God had taken me in and comforted me with his love and brought us back together. I didn't have a plan when I started writing, but I ended up writing down my proposal to her. It ended with:

So today, with all my heart, with everything I have, and with you by my side, I ask you: Will you be my wife—forever and always? Let me be your forever love as long as I live?

Will you marry me?

I sat there and looked at the notebook page, the backside of where I had started an hour earlier. I flexed my right hand from cramps and took a sip of my beer. That was it. That was my proposal. I had to ask her now. The ring was upstairs in the hotel room, tucked into a secret compartment in my backpack. I waited for a text that she was awake, which came a few moments later. In customary form, she merely texted, "Hi."

"Hi," I said, my fingers trembling with nervous excitement. "Sleep well?"

"I think. Maybe only a few minutes but enough. Are you coming up or have more work to do?" she asked.

Are you kidding? I thought. I was in the elevator before I could even finish reading her second text.

"I'm heading up now," I wrote.

She sent me back a kissing emoji just as I was getting off the elevator on the sixth floor.

I turned left, walked past three hotel room doors, and arrived at ours. *It's now been over twenty-one years since I asked her to marry me. I'm doing it again, for real, with a ring the size of Gibraltar!* I thought. I took a deep breath, prayed quickly—or rather thanked God for her—and pressed the room key against the reader. *Click!* went the lock.

Phew. Here we go.

"Hi, baby," she said, propped up on a few pillows on the bed.

"Hi, love," I replied.

My hands never sweat, even when I'm sweating, but they were sweating then. I knew she would say yes. But would she say yes merely a year after getting back together?

"Get work done?" she asked.

"What? Oh, no, not really," I said as I made a lunge as I walked past my backpack on the floor to get the ring box in one slick motion.

"No? Why not, baby?"

"Well, I ended up writing something. Can I read it to you?"

"Sure. Now?"

"Yeah, kinda. Is that okay?"

"Yeah." She put down her phone and looked me in the eyes.

I couldn't help it; I just started tearing up. I cleared my throat.

"*Baby*. What's wrong?"

"Nothing, love. I'm okay. Here, let me read this," I said.

I proceeded to read the note I had written downstairs, pausing for sniffles, to collect myself, or to see her reaction. She was smiling but had no idea what was coming. She grabbed my left hand with her right and squeezed tightly.

I got to the last few lines and had to stop. Tears were streaming down my face. I couldn't even look at her. I managed somehow to get the last few words out of my mouth: "Will you marry me?"

I looked up. Tears were now streaming down her face, too. I held up the ring box that I had nestled on the other side of me from where she was lying, opened it, and showed it to her.

"Yes!" she said. "Yes, of course, I will!"

"I love you," I said. "You've changed my life."

"You've changed mine. I love you so much!" was her reply.

We kissed, and I gave her an immense hug, a "squeeze hug,"

as my daughter would say, the kind you feel in your bones.

She lifted her hand up to see it with her ring on. "I love it," she said. "I absolutely love it."

Somewhere in heaven, her dad was smiling, saying, "Now, *now* you can marry her."

29 | OUR BEER AT THREE

"We need to remember that God can use other Christians
at any point in our lives to speak to us."
—Lauren C. Moye

I hadn't even remembered applying to a local Greenville agency when I received an email back asking if I could talk to see if we were a good fit. I remembered it so little, in fact, that I had to Google the domain in the sender's email to see if the company would jog my memory. No luck. But if someone local wanted to talk to me about hiring me, I was all in.

"Just so you know," said the email, "I like to have a ten-minute phone conversation to see if we're a fit before we plan to get together in person to talk."

That seemed reasonable to me. I hated trying on shoes, too. I'd rather take them home and walk in them, rather than futz around the store, trying on everything. That's what return policies are for.

"Tomorrow morning, okay?" he said at the end of his email.

"Tomorrow sounds great. Talk to you at 10:00 a.m. Looking forward to talking with you," I said. *Whoever you are.*

The next day while sitting in my sunroom, casually watching

the Tour de France on a little TV bolted into the brick, I was working on my laptop, surveying a spreadsheet of 198 jobs to which I had applied. I looked up from my laptop to discuss the options with Jerushah. We could move to Denver, where my two youngest children were living. Or maybe New York City, Austin, Charlotte, Nashville, or Atlanta would be good places to look for work. But then we'd have to worry about how far she was from her children, so nothing seemed like a good fit other than staying in Greenville—even as much as we wanted to have a fresh start together.

I took a break from watching the Tour and reformatting my complicated spreadsheet when at exactly 10:00 a.m., the phone rang.

"Before we begin," said the man, "just know I may have a contractor call me—I know, bad timing—and if so, I may have to cut this short."

"That's completely all right," I said. "I understand."

We chatted about my history and resume, which he had printed and in front of him. Interested in my short tenures at various places in Silicon Valley, he asked me some specific questions.

"It's a really transient market, especially out West—" I began to respond before he suddenly cut me off.

"Oh, hold on. Actually, I have to take this call. We are going to have to cut this short," he said.

"I understand," thinking I had failed the initial test. It was fine; I still wasn't sure exactly what I was applying for. "Thanks for your time."

"No, no, no. I'm sorry you misunderstood. I want to continue this," he emphasized. "But I do need to take this call. Can you meet me tomorrow? Want to have coffee in the morning or beer in the afternoon?"

"Let's do beer," I said because I thought that if we had coffee, he'd have someplace to be for work, but if we had beer? Maybe we could talk longer if he liked me.

"Great. I'll shoot you details over email. See you tomorrow."

The email later that day instructed me to meet at 3:00 p.m. at a brewery in a nearby suburb. When I showed up exactly fifteen minutes early, he was already there, sitting at a picnic table, waiting for me.

That was the first time I ever met Geoff Wasserman.

He is a fifty-something dad, and he drank a dark beer while he furiously took notes about me in a little tan journal. He was gregarious and friendly and asked me tons of questions, from my reasons for moving to Greenville to my accomplishments. He had stalked my LinkedIn profile the day prior and said what he liked most about me was the reviews from my former employees.

"I always start with the people who worked *for* potential candidates," he said. "They are the ones whose opinion matters most."

I still didn't know what I had applied for.

"Thanks," I laughed nervously. "I should go read those again. I can't remember what they say."

Geoff was looking for a "Brand Manager," his name for what most agencies would call an "Account Manager," someone assigned to clients to walk them through all aspects of their projects and needs. His company, The Brand Leader, didn't really need one, he explained, but he kept the opening on the website in case "God brought him someone he wouldn't have found otherwise."

"God?" I asked, probing a bit. It was the South, after all, so you have to wonder here if someone is (a) a churchgoer who merely listens to sermons on Sundays, or (b) someone who genuinely loves Jesus and therefore practices what he hears on Sundays throughout the week.

Geoff was the latter. Raised Jewish in Montreal, he had lived a life full of ups and downs just like me and had come to know Jesus along a not too dissimilar path. He was also divorced with children and remarried to his life's love, who herself had children. Their blended family contained five children in all, and they dealt with the same parental issues with their own exes as I had.

Then I told Geoff my story and, knowing he loved the Lord, went into details about how he had chased me to save me. He nearly cried. (I was starting to get used to this response).

After about an hour and a half of small talk mixed with our life and career stories, he said, "Why don't you start your own agency? You clearly have the ability and the desire."

"But not the capital," I said. "I have to feed my family in the interim. I have nothing to start one with, nor a way to get paid."

"Right," he agreed. "But what if I gave you a blank check to start one."

"*Are* you giving me a blank check?"

"Well, no . . ."

"Then I'm not starting an agency," I said. "Not to sound like a jerk, but this is exactly the issue."

"Ha," he laughed. "Okay, good point."

After some more small talk, he just said simply, "I wonder something."

"Yeah, what's that?" I asked.

"I want to retire in a few years. My kids want to do something else anyway. I've been wondering what to do: close-up shop? Sell? I've been praying about this."

"*Okay—*" I strung out the word, wondering where he was going with this.

"You want an agency one day," he said. He seemed confident, even though I was unsure that was actually my goal. "You want an agency. I have an agency," Geoff said.

"I'm not following, Geoff. Maybe it's the beer." As a light-weight, I could take one IPA, not two. I was on my third.

"Why don't you work with me now, I'll retire or sell you the business in a few years, and in the middle, we make magic together?"

"Wow. What?" I said.

"I'll teach you about running an agency. You teach me about digital marketing and e-commerce. We build an amazing business, and then one day, it's yours."

I had heard this before. "When you turn sixteen, 'The Mouse' is yours." I was skeptical, and he was in no rush to map out his business on the back of a beer napkin.

"Let's think about it and pray about it," said Geoff. "Then maybe get together again to talk some more about it."

I thought that meant our time was over, but we sat for another hour and a half, talking about our lives, our wives, our children, and how we grew up.

I left at about 6:30 p.m. We had sat and talked for three and half hours about so much. It wasn't a job interview; it wasn't an offer. It was an adult, thoughtful conversation about what I was meant to do in this life, professionally. God had sent men to invest in me in different areas but never someone to invest in me professionally. But something was clicking. God's tumblers were moving into position. "'For I know the plans I have for you,' declares the LORD, 'plans to prosper you and not to harm you, plans to give you hope and a future.'" (Jer 29:11).

I had been shown the plan for my life in every way but a career. I was fearful that no matter the position I would eventually accept, I would slip back into my old persona. If I was going to be working, it should be for someone like Geoff. A Jewish guy who could read the Hebrew on my leg as well as my body language. He was the closest I had seen to Jesus in the workplace.

"Plans to give you hope and a future," I thought. I hadn't realized his plan was on-going, that it didn't end with my new commitment to Christ or after finding my one true love. It would last much longer than that.

Geoff and I met again a few days later unexpectedly because we enjoyed the conversation so much. I met him at a temporary workspace while his new building was still under construction. We sat on the patio in two old Adirondack chairs and picked up right where we had left off.

"Have you given any more thought to what we talked about?" Geoff said.

"About you giving me a blank check? Yes."

We laughed, knowing the absurdity of the idea. But it broke any ice that may have formed in the hours since I had seen him.

That went on for a while: meeting at random times—and often—to talk about the future. We never spoke specifically about roles, but we talked around everything else. I had no idea he was grooming me to be his number two.

For about six weeks, we talked, prayed, thought, and spoke to our wives. Our wives even met each other when the four of us all went out to dinner to see if we could all, what we call, "get along." Later, he would tell me that was a test to see how I treated people like wait staff and others. I passed, although I wouldn't have just a few years prior. Our wives instantly clicked, and the conversation was natural and fun.

Lastly, I met Chris, Geoff's longtime employee and current creative director. He had worked for The Brand Leader for eleven years and had grown up there—it was his first job out of college. He was a little awkward, a little backwoods South Carolina, but charming and authentic, not to mention incredibly talented. Chris and I met at a taco shop where he peppered me with questions:

"How was it at Nike?"

"Where have you traveled?"

"How many people worked for you?"

"What was it like at a start-up?"

These were hard to answer because answering him only reminded me of my past, who I had hurt, how I had tried only to get ahead, and the shame that all had brought.

"Man, you've done so much!" he said. "You're so cool." Chris had a little man-crush on me, which I needed to squash.

Chris had gone to Liberty University, so I assumed he was a believer and asked him some questions that confirmed this assumption. Being bold in my new faith, I offered to bless our meal and talked candidly to him about my failures. I also spoke about how the Lord had saved me—twice. It seemed to go well.

Then out of the blue, in the parking lot after lunch, he said, "Can I ask you a personal question?"

Uh-oh, I thought. Here it comes. The "divorce" question.

"You've been around lots of companies and done and seen lots of things," said Chris.

"Yeah . . ." I responded, wondering where this was going.

"Is my . . . you know . . ." he said hesitantly. "Is my work . . . any good?"

I was dumbfounded. Here was this seemingly confident, mature, super-talented Christ-follower asking me if he was any good?

"Chris, let me be honest with you. I've seen your work, okay? I've also been in the room when we hired some of the biggest agencies in the United States through my work at Dr. Martens, Nike, and Keen."

He was expecting an answer he feared the most.

"Your," I said, pointing to his chest. "Your work? It's at the same level as—if not better than—their creative directors."

"It is?" he said surprisingly.

"One hundred percent," I assured him. "But here's the problem. The fact that you even have to ask me that question is why you've never been invited into that room."

He wasn't sure how to respond. Was he good, or wasn't he? I understood why he was asking; I had dealt with my fair share of imposter syndrome, but this guy was good. I truly hadn't seen work like his at any level. Even if he feigned confidence, something I was good at, he'd be killing it.

"I can't teach design, Chris. But I can teach confidence," I said. "Let's get you in that room. You belong there."

His smile said everything. Now I was hoping that I could actually deliver.

A few weeks later, Geoff offered me a job, which I had to turn down due to the money.

"This is all I can do," he said on a phone call after he emailed the offer letter.

"I get that," I said, "but I can't pay my bills at that rate. It's just . . . math."

"I don't know how else to get us there."

"I want to make this work, but between getting married, the house, and my kids' child support, I can't make that work. I'm sorry."

He said he'd think about it and call me back. An hour later, he called and said, "Can you meet me for a beer?"

"Of course," I replied, "but I'm bringing my wife."

As we sat and talked openly at the nearby Universal Joint pub, he said, "I'm just going to put this out there. I wasn't expecting to hire my 'Kyle' right now. You're about six months too early. But it's not my timing; it's God's." He looked up to the ceiling—to heaven. Then he looked at me again. "I'm afraid if I pass on you, you won't be available in six months."

"I won't be," I cut him off. "I have about two months of savings before I collapse. I'll find something."

"What do you need to live?" he asked, "down to the penny."

"I can put a super tight budget together for you," I said.

"Great," said Geoff. Then he finished the last third of his beer in one long swallow. "Do that and get it to me tonight."

Jerushah and I worked on that budget so meticulously we could've figured out how to bring the Apollo 13 astronauts back; it was so detailed. When we were done, she said, "That's our number."

I relayed it to Geoff.

"Then that's what I'll give you," he replied. "I'll draw it up."

Jerushah and I looked at each other. *God's plan. Not ours.*

When the offer came through—not even half of my paycheck at Dr. Martens—we were elated. Well, all but one thing. I called Geoff back.

"The contract says we have to be at work at 8:15 a.m. daily," I said.

"Yeah, that's when the office opens."

"I'm not trying to be a prima donna or anything, but it takes an act of God to get me into the office before 9:00 a.m. I work hard, but I can't do that—I like to work out and then take my time coming in. I'll give you twice the amount of work in the same time it takes anyone else, but—"

"Okay," he said. "Cross that out and sign it. We have a deal."

I did just that, with a few more adjustments: I was going to work part-time through August because we were getting married on Labor Day, September 1, 2019. I'd start full-time when I returned from my honeymoon.

My first two weeks of any job, I had always felt incredibly uncomfortable and stupid, like I had duped them somehow or someone had lost a bet and I was the consolation prize. The vocabulary was always the thing that got my imposter syndrome started. Every company's vernacular was just different enough, tailored enough to fit their culture, that any knowledge I had when I walked in was out-dated or worse—wrong. Those first few days were exhausting as my brain was rewiring itself to link old words to new words, learning definitions, and grappling with entirely new concepts.

In the 1990 Tony Scott film *Days of Thunder*, starring Tom Cruise as a cocky NASCAR driver, there is a scene where the head mechanic, Harry, played by Robert Duvall, is trying to form a rela-tionship with Cruise's character, Cole Trickle. It seems like good ol' Cole doesn't listen well to Duvall's coaching, and as a result, is burn-ing up his tires and losing vital time. They need to figure something out to communicate to be able to succeed.

Harry pulls up next to Cole at the bar, "We've got to talk," he said.

"All right, talk," Cole replies.

"On the radio during the race," starts Harry, "You wanna run right on the ragged edge all the damn time. You gotta tell me what's going on with the car!"

"You want to change the way I drive," says Cole sternly.

"Maybe," says Harry honestly.

"Maybe you could set up the car so I don't have to change."

Surprised, Harry says, "I'd be happy to—you just tell me how."

"What do you want to know?" says Cole.

"Hell, Cole, you're the driver. If you think she's runnin' loose or soft, tell us—we give a turn here, take some wedge out there—we'll win some races. That's all there is to it."

"I can't do that."

"Why the hell not?" asks Harry, now angry.

"Because I don't know what the fuck you're talking about!"

Puzzled, Harry says, "How do you mean that?"

Cole looks around to make sure no one is looking. "I mean, I really don't know what you just said about a turn there or a wedge there. I don't know."

"How did that happen?"

"What's the difference?" reacts Cole. "They told me to get in the car and drive, and I could drive, okay? The point is, I'd like to help, but I can't. I'm an idiot. I don't have the vocabulary."

"Then we'll just have to figure one out."

This was how I felt when I started a new job. It didn't matter if I was painting for my father as a child, editing articles for *Inside Triathlon*, or running the entire international e-commerce department at Dr. Martens. Now, at Geoff's agency, I was hearing words that I didn't know what they meant: brand guidelines, positioning, archetypes. *Idiot!* I didn't have the vocabulary.

This was how I felt most of my life as a Christian, too—when I was actually *trying* to be a Christian. I had no Christian vocabulary to ask the questions I needed. I was embarrassed to ask. Should I pray out loud or to myself? On my knees or anywhere? Were my eyes supposed to be closed? I wasn't talking about the Christian bookstore-type Christian who wanted to quote "Footsteps in the Sand" and say the right thing in church on Sundays. I was talking about right now, *in Christ,* what was the vocabulary?

With Geoff, the vocabulary didn't matter. Not in the agency, not in life, and not in our blossoming friendship. With him, I had the freedom to learn and mess up. I didn't have to have a perfect vocabulary or the correct answers. He took me, imperfections and all, and saw me for who I was. In a way, he was the business version of Jerushah: took me as he found me, let me become who I was trying to be, and loved on me as best as he was able. While he wasn't a father figure to me, he was a man who showed me how to be a father. How to love and be loved.

That solid acceptance—and his six weeks of due diligence—proved him right. I was able to slide into a role that felt tailor-made for me. Through God's providence, I not only earned a right to be in Geoff's company but in his trust circle as well.

Geoff also quickly and easily had permission to speak into my life. He tells me when my own thoughts of my value are completely wrong and off-base. He also tells me when I'm slipping back to my old self, but he works with me, not just in the business, but on my journey to be the man Jesus hoped for me. Sometimes that means we argue and fight; most of the time, however, it means we choose to understand that the Lord created us both—yes, in his own image—to be who we are and to help refine one another. Someone once told me that if we take Proverbs 27:17 seriously ("As iron sharpens iron, so one person sharpens another"), then we can expect sparks to occasionally fly when we're bumping steel in hopes of honing each other. I had never had someone in my life who not only had the desire and ability to speak into my life but who himself also wanted a similar partner.

Time will tell if I own part or all of the business in the future. It's certainly a desire and hope from my end, but it's either in God's plan or not. One thing, however, is clear: God brought Geoff into my life to show me—from the business side—that I am valuable. I am worthy. God, once again, had used a Jewish-born man to show me about Jesus.

God's plan. Not ours.

30 | TROPHIES OF GRACE

"Ladies and gentlemen, will you please stand?
With every guitar string scar on my hand,
I take this magnetic force of a man to be my . . . lover.
My heart's been borrowed and yours has been blue
All's well that ends well to end up with you."
—Taylor Swift, "Lover"

The big day had finally arrived, September 1, 2019. We decided to have a small ceremony with a few of our closest friends and some family at a rooftop restaurant overlooking downtown Greenville. Jerushah wore a sleeved wedding dress, her hair perfectly half-tied back from the sides and the rest gently falling on her shoulders and then some. Jerushah, the kids, and I all wore Vans SK8-Lows of varying colors. She chose a baby blue pair for her something blue. I opted for a dark-brown suede to complement my suit.

From my family, I had only invited my brother and sister, but I called upon a few old friends from afar: Scott from Seattle, Troy from Portland, and Grant from Denver, who couldn't make it. Jerushah's longtime girlfriends—including Olivia (the friend who was there when I had first met Jeru in Boulder) and her husband.

There were seven gay men there, all dear friends of ours. Three of our six children were there, and our good friend, Robbie, of course, was our "Man of Honor." So many interesting people representing marginalized groups that it was like a gathering of circus carnies.

Gigi, my mother-in-law, quipped, "I feel like I'm in a scene from *The Greatest Showman!*"

Some of Jerushah's siblings were in attendance: her older—and only—sister, Berdjette, and her husband, David. Aram, her closest brother, walked her down the aisle, and one of her other brothers, Tullian, presided over the ceremony. There was no one else we even considered.

Tullian was twenty-three when I had first met him. Only two years older than me, he was already a charismatic preacher and doing well, by both the world's and the church's standards.

Post-seminary, he had launched his pastoral career of which many would be jealous. He had a very large congregation and, along with the benefits of a large church, had sold numerous books and was on the speaking circuit, both live and on TV. He was the founding pastor of the former New City Church in Fort Lauderdale, Florida, which ended up merging with the historic Coral Ridge Presbyterian Church in 2009. He then served there as the senior pastor and would routinely preach to over ten thousand people. For all intents and purposes, he had become the celebrity pastor he wanted to be.

When I first met him, he was brash and cocky. I would often say that out of all of Jerushah's brothers, he was probably the most prickly. When I was first engaged to his sister, he didn't pay much attention to us. Twenty years later, he would barely remember my name when I came back into her life. That was just who he was: selfish. He loved the pedestal on which people had propped him up and enjoyed the spotlight. He claimed to love Jesus—and I don't doubt that he did—I just didn't know if he would say he actually *knew* him.

It's a gift to be able to look at your own faults, to see your own need for redemption, and not only move forward but then allow your own pain, suffering, and shame to lead others to the Lord. Tullian has shown me—and countless others, including his sister—wild grace, compassion, understanding, and love. Today, show me a redeemed man and I'll show you my brother-in-law.

But it wasn't always that way. He married young to a beautiful woman who loved and admired him. Together, they had built a great home, had three children, and seemed set. With a large mega-church congregation along with his other side pursuits of writing and speaking, he was also financially set. They looked, to the outside world, like the perfect Christian pastor's family; they had it all together and were held up as the epitome of what Christian life should look like.

Then it all crashed and burned quickly in 2015.

Through a series of events, including infidelity, he lost his marriage, his church, his home, his book deals, and speaking engagements. Tullian was a country song come to life. His world was upended, and he fell flat on his face—hard.

He surfaced at a new church just six months later before a second affair had come to light. After first denying it, he admitted his guilt and sin, was fired again, and decided to come clean. He sat down and admitted all his sins to his wife and—hardest of all—to his young children.

He fought it. His anger boiled. He was pissed off at God, at the world, at the people who had wronged him. He tried to save himself by running from it all. It was in that moment that the Lord started to make something of his situation through offering what he always does, his wild grace.

Without his church, his best-selling books, or his image,

who was Tullian? He didn't know. His image to the world was gone, and since he hung his Christianity on how it made him look, he was further from God than he ever thought possible.

Jesus, however, did something remarkable for us all. He doesn't need our strength, courage, accolades, or performance. What he did—*his* victory—is all we need. No matter what we do, it does not diminish, relinquish, or extinguish what he has done for us. He did it for Tullian. He did it for me. And he does it for you.

Here's the craziest thing: through all of that, he became a completely different man. He's a better father, a better brother, a better pastor. And through his brokenness, God gave him his current wife, Stacie, who herself was redeemed through grace, and now, together, they're better spouses to each other.

He now sends me random texts like, "I love you, brother," with a heart emoji. I guess he remembers my name now.

Tullian finally understands who Jesus really is, has accepted his grace, and has become the man of God he always knew he could be. I believe Jesus is now using him in the lives of other people, including his sister's—my wife—and mine. In a world that sees Christians as self-serving people who stand above the crowd, Tullian is swimming against the current upstream to fight for the marginalized, criticized, and the broken. Like Jesus would've done, he doesn't merely preach to the man in the crowd; he meets him where he needs to be met. He would much rather be with people who are unsure of what they believe and where they belong than the ones who claim it but don't know Jesus.

So, we had no one else in mind to officiate our wedding. He called us both "trophies of grace," that is, items to show to the world that God has redeemed us. We are the light in the broken world that God can use *because* he died for us, showing us grace and mercy.

Recently, when another former pastor, noted for his particular hatred of Tullian and public shaming of him in the aftermath of his affair, was similarly caught in extramarital sin, he called Tullian and apologized. Because Tullian is the man who he is today, he not only took the call but loved on him like Jesus would.

When we're naked and ashamed, God still loves us. He takes our call. We are still trophies of his grace. My brother-in-law has taught me that and taught me to love the ones who are hard to love and to be even more like Jesus to them.

"And now, Jerushah and Kyle have prepared their own vows," Tullian said.

Jerushah started first. "Life is funny, isn't it? I could never imagine the twists and turns and ups and downs that would land us in this place and in this moment. I am grateful. I am grateful that you are here with me. I am grateful that your own ups and downs formed a trail that brought you here to me. I am grateful that I tried to witness to you twenty years ago. I am grateful you met Dad and he loved you.

"I am grateful that you have gray hair and that you will always choose a Friday night *Dateline* over a late night out. I am grateful that your strengths complement my weaknesses in a way that I am free to be myself more than I ever have. But mostly, I am grateful, Kyle, that you do not encourage me to look to you, but to look to the Lord, and you are willing to always be a tool to help push me toward him."

Now she was crying. I was crying. Most of our guests were crying, but she continued, "You do not highlight your goodness to me but encourage me to see *his* goodness. Today, I can make you promises about always being kind and always putting your needs first, but life has taught me that without him, we are incapable of loving each other the way he intends. So I promise you this—I will seek him and that he will enable me to love you, and only you, unconditionally as my sweet husband for the rest of my life. I do not want these words to be a speech that sounds good on this special day. I vow that these words will be words that come to life in the day-to-day journey of our marriage."

"Kyle, you are my *exhale*. You are my happy place and my home. What would be my vows without Taylor Swift? 'My heart's been borrowed, and yours has been blue. But all's well that ends well, to end up with you.'

"I love you."

I wasn't sure how I could follow that, but I tried. I had to wipe my tears and sniffle up my emotions. First, though, I looked at her. She was beautiful. I had to kiss her on the spot, though it wasn't that time in the ceremony.

"Hey," said Tullian, "it's not time yet."

Our guests laughed a low laugh that broke the emotions of everyone crying.

I wiped the remaining tears from my face and pulled out my vows from the chest pocket of my navy-blue suit and started reading. "Jerushah, you ended with Taylor Swift, so it's fitting for me to start with Johnny Cash," I said impromptu.

"Johnny Cash said about his wife, June, that he 'fell into a burning ring of fire.' It was because his undying love for her was so fierce and fiery—so full of passion—that he couldn't describe it any other way. That was true for me in 1997, with a young, fiery Jerushah with whom I instantly fell in love—but it wasn't meant to be then. I had imagined a life of love and longevity and happiness the last twenty-two years that I finally get to have.

"When your father gave us his blessing but added, 'But not yet,' we thought he meant next summer, not in two decades. But I found you again, and I instantly rekindled that flame that always burned for you.

"We share everything from the love we have for all our children to the love of silly things like Jeeps and fall, or better yet, Jeeps in fall. We believed Clive Owen should've been James Bond and that Adnan is innocent. That there's nothing better than a good episode of *Dateline* and a killer charcuterie board. Even our morning coffee—with Splenda, not sugar.

"But you have shown me how to love. How to live. How to be kind, authentic, honest, brave, and courageous. You have shown me what a strong woman of integrity and passion looks like—from standing up to presidents on CNN to loving our friends who have been battered and bruised. You have helped me grow as a man, father, friend, and now—husband. You have loved me through my mistakes and encouraged me in my growth.

"You have completely changed my life. I promised you I'd swim to meet you when the sharks were circling. I promise today to always swim with you—in the choppy, shark-infested waters.

"You are the air I breathe. My hope and joy. My true partner. My equal. My best friend.

"You know me. Everything about me, and you still love me. No one on earth or in heaven moves me like you do, who guides me and strengthens me like you do. I am so grateful, thankful, and honored to do this life with you.

"I promise to love you and care for you forever. To cherish our good times and learn from the rough ones. To never stop pursuing you or fight for us. I promise to cherish you and respect you in all things. I promise to *always* include you in my life—in all things. When I feel or excited, you're by my side, and I, too, will be by yours. I promise to always get you Diet Cokes in the morning or Vitamin Waters at night. To fill your third cup of coffee when you wait for mine to run out, so I have to go anyway. To watch reality TV with you or to cancel CycleBar at the last minute. And I promise to love you with that burning fire forever and always.

"You, Jerushah, are my *everything*. I adore you. And I'm so honored that today I get to call you my wife. Because you've always been my *home*.

"So, baby, fuck it. I love you. Always."

We both used *Dateline*. I thought that was amazing.

When Tullian then said, we—Jerushah and I—were trophies of grace, it finally hit me. God had made me in his image, his son had died for me, and then he had made himself known to me through so many people so I could not only know him but show others through my actions.

God works with broken people. He delights in fixing, reclaiming, and giving new purpose to them. Remember our friend David? Well, God calls him "a man after my own heart."

We all have a story. Yours may feel worse than mine. It may seem better. But when God breaks us—from David down to you and me—we have no choice but to respond and bend a knee.

Then Tullian simply said, "I now pronounce you husband and wife."

Elation. Happiness. *So this is what it feels like,* I thought.

"Now. *Now*. You may kiss your wife," said her brother.

EPILOGUE | Pop Music
"This morning, with her, drinking coffee."
—Johnny Cash

These days, I spend my mornings drinking coffee in bed with my wife in our home in Greenville for a few hours each day watching the *TODAY Show* and enjoying each other's company, all before we workout together, take the kids to school, and head off to work. I enjoy simple, fun things in life now. Things that I had always thought were frivolous, but now I see the joy in—Taylor Swift songs, The *Bachelor/ette*, Diet Coke, Folgers coffee, Forever 21, and Bud Light Lime in the summertime. I even started liking some country music—some, mind you, I'm not crazy. Things I once looked down upon I now see as joyous.

As a result, I laugh more, I cry more, and yeah, I enjoy pop culture. I can laugh at myself and let my kids tease me about being "so old." ("Did you even have indoor plumbing as a child?" they ask, then laugh.) I try to *feel* things now. It's not always easy, but it's worth it.

My mother-in-law, Virginia ("Gigi"), lives in Black Mountain, North Carolina, an hour or so from us and not far from where she grew up in her famous father's home. Interstate 40 runs right between her current home and her childhood one. She told me that when the lines on I-40 started to fade a few years ago, the number of accidents started to increase along that stretch of road. People merging onto the highway couldn't see the merge lane, and those moving at full-speed—but changing lanes—found it hard to stay in their own. The minute they repainted the lane lines, the number of accidents dropped immediately.

We all need lanes in our life to keep us focused and to keep us from wandering off the road, or worse, getting into an accident. The best way for me to do that is by trying to read a verse or a chapter of scripture each morning or by doing a short devotional. That, plus focusing on my partner and her needs, helps me stay in my lane. She also focuses on mine.

I can tell the days that I'm busy, or I forget to start off by reading the Word. I'm more irritable, agitated, restless, and anxious. There's something about reading God's Word that literally soothes my soul as I go about my day.

I have other lane lines, too, that help guide me. I share everything with my wife. That promise we made still holds: *Honest always, even when hard.* That has never wavered. We have access to each other's phones, email, and social media. Not because we don't trust each other, but because we have nothing to hide. It's so nice to know I'm so real and authentic with my wife—and in my life—that I don't live in fear of anything she may find on my iPhone. There's nothing in which I'm ashamed. I also tell her my fears, anxieties, and struggles—because I still have them—and together, we work through them.

I'm also trying to develop more relationships with good men in my life. Many of whom we've talked about here. These men are there for me, and me for them. We're able to share the challenges of fatherhood, work, or faith. Some of the men we talked about are unaware that since we crossed paths, I have changed my life and re-committed myself to Christ. I hope I have the chance to apologize to them in person for the guy I was to them in my past; they're out there somewhere. Email me if you read this.

For the ones I still know, I'm happy to report they are doing well. Ryan just sent me a photo of all of us riding bikes in 1983. Josh is still a friend and living as a lawyer in Michigan with his wife and three kids. (He recently sent me a great Liege waffle recipe that I use on Sundays to make waffles for our family.) I've lost touch with people like Mike, Major Matt, some of the AGO brothers, as well as many of those present during my climbing accident. But many of them are still around and are dear friends: Alan, Frank, Chum, Lance, Wally, and, of course, Tullian and Aram.

Brian, the Xerox man, and I recently spoke after what seemed like twenty years. His sons long grown, he was still in the same house he had moved to in the eighties, happily retired with his wife by his side.

"I was happy to fill in for your father," he told me. "He didn't realize what a remarkable young man he had on his hands." Later in our conversation, he reminded me, "God has been placing fathers in your path your whole life, and ultimately, you ended up with the heavenly kind." Amen, Brian.

My real father died in 2005, with his last wife, Maggie, and his sister, Bonnie, by his side. When I reconnected with Bonnie to ask about him at the prompting of my therapist in 2018, I was floored by a story she told me: "Your father didn't want to die in a hospital," she said. "He wanted to be at home. Well, in his final days, I'd come over and we'd sit on an old porch swing he built. I'd hold his hand as we stared into the field. Maggie would wrap him in a blanket and we'd just sit there for hours. It was the day or so before he passed that he squeezed my hand after a long while of silence, and he turned to me with tears in his eyes. He said, "Do you think Kyle knows how proud of him I am?'" she said. "I told him, absolutely." I've found pleasure in learning of the man he wanted to be.

My mother retired and lives in Eastern Tennessee, about a three-hour drive from us. We'll meet up every summer so she can visit with the children, all of them, but we've never been too close.

My brother moved to Morocco to continue his career at the late age of fifty-seven, and he's so happy he'll retire there. My sister, however, made the biggest change of her life and moved to Los Angeles with her husband—neither of them having ever lived west of Pittsburgh.

What's next? I'm still running the race left before me, but I've applied lessons I've learned about running to my spiritual journey, too. I have run since I was little—sometimes I'm good at it, sometimes I'm not. I was decently fast in my twenties, horribly slow in my thirties, and now in my forties, I have found a new rhythm that I never thought I'd be able to have at my age. Even so, I tend to have good days and bad days. Sometimes I can rip off a half dozen miles at blazing speed (for me), and other times—*most times*—I struggle to even want to lace up my shoes.

During seasons of training for something—a half-marathon or 10K—I find myself more focused when I have a goal. I plan my runs meticulously, down to the time of day, my target heart rate zone, and pace. I also look holistically over a season to see when I'll be in peak form for a hard training day or for the race itself. On most days that I run, my wife and I run together, and she's equally competitive.

When you run, the best way to be more efficient is to look ahead, toward the horizon. You're faster that way, too. But as a data-driven geek (I track my heart rate, its variability, sleep, and calories), I tend to focus on my Apple Watch as I run. Even if it's merely every stride or two, it takes my eyes off the horizon and I tend to slow down.

Phil Cassanta, an old friend and coach from my triathlon days, once told me, "You know, each time you look down and worry about your pace, you slow down and pull yourself *off* your pace. Stop looking down and look *forward!* That's how you go faster."

If I set a goal and keep looking up, that's when I keep advancing in my life and faith.

Paul constantly speaks of our life in Christ as the race (Gal 5:7, 2 Tim 4:7, Phil 2:16, Acts 20:24). We're all in the race of life. How are we running it? Are we moving fast and furious for ourselves, looking down at our time, trying to best our personal record? Or are we running along swiftly, eyes forward, looking up toward Christ without worrying about our days but looking to him for guidance?

Looking forward, or looking up, is an act of focusing on God's wisdom for us. When we look down, Paul says we are looking at the world, and the wisdom that's of the world, which God knows is how we shouldn't live. But we need to look up and look at Christ. A long time ago, back in 1994, I heard an interview with musician Charlie Peacock, on the end of one of his records. He said, "I guess if we believe that if Jesus is really at the center of our life, then he's at the center of our dreams and imaginings as well . . . I think anything less is a little less human and a lot less of what God has called us to be." Then he referenced Eugene Peterson's *Message* translations of Colossians 3:1:

> "So if you're serious about living this new resurrection life with Christ, *act* like it. Pursue the things over which Christ presides. Don't shuffle along, eyes to the ground, absorbed with the things right in front of you. Look up, and be alert to what is going on around Christ—*that's* where the action is. See things from *his* perspective."

I try to see things from his perspective these days (God's,

not Charlie's), and I definitely have kept my deal with him—never to deny him again. I also take great courage in reading the scriptures these days, and I've also found great delight in learning about David. If there was one person who knew brokenness, it was him. In his youth, he was a brave young man who slew the giant Philistine, Goliath, with a slingshot—and a dose of God's help. He became a decorated war hero and then eventually king of his country. Having committed adultery, murdered, lied, and covered it up, he then got his punishment from the Lord—he was broken down before God. Yet his testimony reminds us that when we are penitent before the Lord, in an honest and broken way, he will certainly renew a right spirit in us. (Ps. 51:10)

I was made in the image of God, just like David, and just like you. Broken men can still be used to their fullest extent. Jacob could become Israel only when he was broken. Moses could become a leader and a prophet only when he was broken. Jesus couldn't take our sins on himself at the cross unless he, too, was broken—literally—for mankind.

In my life, I've worn masks a lot: for work, for college, for relationships, for family, and for friendships. When someone once quipped to me that they didn't even know the "real Kyle," my response was, "I don't even know the real me!"

But Jesus always did. He never doubted, and he put those people in my life to forever guide me back to him, with all their baggage, bumps, and bruises. He loved me as I was, but without coming to terms with myself that I could be loved as well, I just couldn't fully appropriate myself to him.

Are you feeling that way right now? Are you feeling like you're unknown or don't know how to appropriate yourself to God? Do you feel broken? I encourage you to ask God for help. Ask him to enter your heart—for the first, second, or umpteenth time. I promise you it gets better. I promise you because he, Jesus, promises you it will. Tullian often preaches that "The sins you can't seem to forget, God doesn't remember." So what do you have to lose?

Bring your baggage, your brokenness, your trepidation, your darkness, your secrets; bring it all to the foot of Jesus. Maybe you'll simply scream at him like I did. Go ahead! He won't be deterred. He's not going anywhere. Curse at him. Yell at him. Or quietly speak to him—but do talk to him. If you're quiet enough in your heart and spirit, you just might hear him reply. He'll certainly be listening.

The toughest, boldest men I know are that way because of Jesus (Bear Grylls comes to mind). They walk unafraid because they walk in his light. So, if you, too, wish to be like them, it's as easy as A-B-C: accept he died for you, believe he is who he says he is, and commit your life to knowing him. Not in the cheesy sense. No one is saying you have to listen only to old 1970's Keith Green records and grow your hair long. But *really* decide you'll follow who he is and who he said he was. Commit yourself to being like him. That doesn't necessarily mean be like church leaders or everyone who professes to know him. When you're confused, see what he did . . . and do the same. Live like you love him, love others, and you'll be better for it.

No matter what you decide, you'll be welcome at our table. But if you decided to follow Jesus, or recommit your life to him, tell somebody. Your pastor, or friends, and your spouse or loved ones. And tell me, too. You can find my email at the end of this book.

ACKNOWLEDGMENTS

There are a few people in my life in which I now can tell in hindsight God put in my path for a reason, to make me better, stronger, wiser, and more the man I was made to be. I owe my life to these few, but amazing, men: André Berard, Joshua Creem, Alan Braem, Lance Knight, Brian Wildes, Matt Hamilton, Craig DeMartino, John Toggas, Jesse Stainbrook, Greg Leisinger, Dave Geipel, Erik Boldt, Adam Blaisdell, Ken Pierce, Dave Bechtold, Rick Mattson, Gerry Chapeau, Dave Geipel, Ray Donatucci, Ken Tankersley, Scott Brase, John-Eric Travis, Nate Emhoff, Frank DePentino, Paul Borth, Scott Downing, Jonah Werner, "Big Paul" Myers, John Nunez, Chris "Wally" Olson, Scott Hayzlett, Chum Wongrassame, Bobby Kennedy, Brent Koel, Chris Alber, Andy Hawk, Rick Rundall, Grant Davis, Scott Schumaker, Tim Moxey, Kyle Goodrich, Pér Flood, Matt Bean, Mark Lemma, Paul Razo, Mark Galbraith, Nick Lawrence, Troy Kent, Shorin Nemeth, Sam McKee, Tom O'Leary, Matt Daniel, Walker MacWilliam, Antony and Tullian Tchividjian, Robbie Randolph, Brock Meadows, Joe Hindman, Ryne Brown, Greg Dover, Tim Lowry, Rich Hefty, Chris Heuvel, Geoff Wasserman, and Brent Warwick. Thank you all for showing me how to be a friend, father, husband, colleague, employee (and employer), man of faith, and man of strength—all in your own way.

A huge thanks to Charlie Peacock for agreeing on a random Saturday morning in July, through a Twitter direct message of all things, to write his foreward. I am so grateful for your music and kindness (not in that order).

Thank you, especially to Geoff Wasserman, for allowing me to use resources and time to complete this and to Jenna Fant for the first round of editing at all times of the day or night.

A big thank you to Stephanie De Arman for agreeing to put the final polish on this with all ~~you're~~ your skills of book editing and for your friendship to my wife and me. "Writing!" (Said with thumbs in the air!)

To Chris Heuvel, where do I start? You have quickly become one of my favorite people. Your remarkable commitment to making this book's cover unlike any other I will never be able to thank you enough for. You are the most talented designer I've ever known.

To my brother, Christian, and sister, Allyson. I love you both shoom-shoom, and I'm thankful I got to go through life with both of you at various times. A special thanks to Aram Tchividjian: You are my brother in Christ, in family, and in friendship. I love you, man.

To my children, Logan, Jackson, Morgan, Anabelle, Liam, and Ali—thank you for your persistence, passion, and perseverance. I love you all, and I'm proud to be your dad. May the Lord bless the six of you in ways I could never even dream—but have prayed for.

Of course, I am *nothing* without my wife, Jerushah. You are my life, my love, my hope, and my joy. You changed my life, baby. I'm so thankful we found each other again. Always and forever will I love you.

ABOUT THE AUTHOR

KYLE DUFORD is the Executive Creative Director of The Brand Leader in Greenville, South Carolina. He is a former magazine editor and writer who turned to branding, as well as a speaker and thought leader. He prides himself on being a husband and father first, an athlete second, and then he works to help create unforgettable brands at The Brand Leader with some of his favorite people. He lives with his wife and—depending on the season—varying numbers of their six children and two dogs.

kyleduford.co
Instagram: @yeahthatkyle
Twitter: @kyleduford
kyleduford@gmail.com